Stock-Flow-Consistent Models and Institutional Variety

Amelia Correa
St Andrew's College, India

Romar Correa
formerly Department of Economics,
University of Mumbai, India

Vernon Series in Economic Methodology

VERNON PRESS

www.vernonpress.com

In the Americas:
Vernon Press
1000 N West Street,
Suite 1200, Wilmington,
Delaware 19801
United States

In the rest of the world:
Vernon Press
C/Sancti Espiritu 17,
Malaga, 29006
Spain

Vernon Series in Economic Methodology

Library of Congress Control Number: 2017942579

ISBN: 978-1-62273-181-7

Table of Contents

To

the Department of Economics

University of Mumbai

Preface

We started out to consolidate our work on the Godley-Cripps-Lavoie (GCL) Stock-Flow-Consistent (SFC) framework but were quickly forced to follow in the footsteps of other giants in political economy who wrote their own pioneering aggregative accounting equations. Depending on sweep and scope, all of the above were captivated by the unfolding of the dynamics of the capitalist economy and as well as the transition of pre-capitalist through capitalist to "casino capitalist" (Susan Strange) forms. To that end, we rearrange GCL identities and highlight the aggregates of interest for chapter and subsection. The special feature of GCL is the postulation of SFC norms, ratios between sub aggregates, some of which connect one period with the next. These ratios are empirical and can, consequently, change across time and space. Our institutional variety includes the concatenation of different such numbers. SFC norms can also be created and imposed and this feature emerges when the issue at hand is one of "stabilizing an unstable economy" (Hyman Minsky).

What about micro foundations? One popular disaggregation of GNP is that between wages and profits. Behind these categories are, naturally, workers and capitalists. The existence and behaviour of these classes is theoretically and statistically problematic when the income of both dwindles as they become better off transmuting into rentiers. Continuing in front of us is the flat trajectory of real activity and the vibrancy of financial activity everywhere in the world. By way of explanation, our research strategy has been to move and shake identities to derive first-order difference equations. Thereafter, we look at the steady state solutions. The classes backing the aggregates interact in conflict or cooperation mode. We set up and solve a series of dynamic games.

The critical comments of two anonymous reviewers went a long way in providing sequence and structure to a first draft that was short on both fronts.

Amelia Correa

Romar Correa

Chapter 1

Introduction

Ever since Kenneth Arrow, along with Samuel Bowles and Herbert Gintis, the latter two having learnt early to straddle the divide between orthodoxy and heterodoxy, removed themselves along with others to the Santa Fe Institute to ponder over political economy as progressive social science, both neoclassical and non neoclassical economists have discovered systems theory. The whole and the parts are connected in mysterious ways. The aggregates that define "higher-level" phenomena have properties not possessed by the "lower-level" individual items that constitute them (Sugden, 2016). System properties combine emergence and, in principle, an unknowable future (Heise, 2016). The proposition connects determinacy in the sense of the connections between system elements, and "downward causation" which states that macro cannot be derived from micro. Emergence is a "brute and unexplainable fact" since there is an ontological gap between the micro and the new property (Brisset, 2016). At the same time, while new arrangements are indispensable to our apparatus, existing arrangements are equally primary as the bases for real agents to choose and act. A related aspect of the systems view is reflexivity in the sense that agents' means act on ends which act on adjusted means in a sequential process (Davis, 2016). That is to say, by transitivity and the cessation of processes through the realisation of ends, means operate on means

Systems theory has developed a battery of concepts to elucidate the hierarchical ordering of the organisational structure of all systems. Apart from lateral connections, there are "supremal units" and "infimal units" with orders going out from 'bosses' to 'workers', so to speak. Power and authority, in other words, are an integral feature of institutions (Dosi et al, 2016; Sakai, 2016). Indeed, the notions are at the heart of the market process. Even members of the Chicago School would not deny that market agents need "control units". With financial arrangements getting more complex, in particular, the demands of central control over banking and currency systems get more urgent. Free banking would reduce stable monetary systems to chaos. A few possess the capacity to determine the choice sets of many. A handful can veto the decisions of millions. Recently, the concept of entropy has been applied to the conceptual armoury of economics (Vozna, 2016). The pioneer was Nicholas Georgesçu-Roegen, another giant who defied categorisation in 'cold war' terms. In the beginning, human labour in agriculture added to the accumulation of the productive potential of society. Work in the form of mechanical and intellectual effort resulted in the growth of transformed energy on the earth. In other words, labour offers the possibility of counteracting entropy or the dissipation of energy.

Individual choices are enmeshed in a skein of multifarious influences which eventually result in "contradictions" underlying a socio-economic system which distinguishes it from a deterministic or stochastic system (Hanappi & Scholz-Waeckerle, 2016; Irwin, 2017). The term suggests, in the first place, the impossibility of identifying all the characteristics of alternative systems and, therefore, of unambiguously specifying utility functions for social choice theory. Secondly, the word suggests the limitations of communicating decisions which entail uncertain costs and benefits to different sections of society over time. For instance, with fiscal policy it is not easy to convey regressive taxation policy or balanced budgets in the light of inter temporal Ricardian equivalence. Lest the complexity approach be seen as a case for nihilism, history provides causal arrows, statistical regularities and constraints that can be identified. So-called "generative structures" exist that are independent of the conditions under which their econometric identification takes place. They are causal mechanisms that are tendencies even though they may never be actualised. Every epoch is a plateau that calls a ceasefire in real contradictions either through their postponement (in time) or through the colonisation of virgin territory (in space). Institutions can be durable as well as assume a life of their own. As culture, they succeed in blocking paths to revolutionary transformation. However, real contradictions cannot be suppressed forever. When the contradictions are grasped by a wide section of the people, the conditions of a tipping point are laid. The denouement must be grasped and reflected upon before the evolutionary jump is made.

Another neglected quiet revolutionary solidly within the mainstream camp whose work bears on our thesis is George Katona. According to him, aggregate phenomena must be seen as social phenomena which do not correspond to individual behaviour (Dechaux, 2014). Unlike Herbert Simon, Katona focussed on macro and unlike the behavioural economics of today, his behavioural economics combined social psychology and *gestalt.* He elucidated the concept of "macrolearning". Individual attitudes and behaviour are a measure of the impact of social mores and conventions on the individual. Katona made the case for a social scientific approach to expectations formation which investigated the origin and transformation of the degrees of confidence of people, their optimism that gave way to pessimism and the more difficult reverse journey (Dechaux, 2015). In short, Katona's perception of the economic process was one in which the judgements of agents and their codes of conduct that followed were central. He distanced himself from the unquestioned assumption that information determined expectations and opted, instead, for the equivalence of expectations and attitudes. Attitudes are points of view widely held that influence perceptions and then behaviour. Katona neatly summarises the concepts in individual thought and action in the following scheme (Dechaux, 2015, p 17). A change in the data or stimulus, S, conditional on a given battery of concepts, X, are filtered through expectations as an intervening variable, I, to determine behaviour R. We have $S/X \rightarrow I \rightarrow R$. There are no functions connecting the three elements. Expectations are orientations towards the future that might change current behaviour. They can be taken as ex ante intervening variables.

In sum, real-world economies consist of "heterogeneous interacting participants" constrained by a changing state of the world (Tesfatsion, 2017). These participants are "locally constructive", that is plan and act on the basis of the markets in which they operate at any point of time. Agents can mean classes. "System constructivity" here means the construction of the state vector by piecing together the dispersed information scalars of different agents. The language of differential games is commonly used to join these elements. The state of the world evolves through a dynamical equation that is driven by classes that, depending on the description of the state vector, may be playing a cooperative or a non cooperative dynamic game. The description of the laws of motion of the system is not unique and neither is the configuration of classes. We will respect the distinction in our survey of political economy in the next chapter. Following in the footsteps of the founding fathers, there will be models best confined to the evocations of national income identities masterfully reconstructed. Our contribution will be to introduce a dynamism from lags (leads) emerging naturally from the definitions. Chapters 2 and 4 offer many such illustrations. On the other hand, there will be Keynesian models that beg microeconomic drivers. Keynes himself relied heavily on the maximum principle in his theorizing. Thus, while Profits are critical, the profit function of the entrepreneur or capitalist will be specified. We will not rely on various formulations of investment functions or posit different consumption or savings propensities.

Our plan of action is to offer dynamical models and pause. They merit scrutiny in their own right as the sometimes surprising fruit of identities. Chapter 3, from a tiny clutch of definitions, comes up with transitional dynamics for a predominantly agrarian economy, on the one hand, and three species of movement for a financially-sophisticated modern economy. The treatment can be regarded as independent of Chapter 6 where all the dynamical systems are regarded as constraints under which appropriate sets of agents operate. The agents introduce themselves from the specification of the equations. Thus, the representative agent is the amalgam of worker and household. Introductory macroeconomic identities can be written for Consumption or Wages. Our procedure to solve out for consumption or wages (lower-case letters) only means that the equivalent other identity is not on the page. The payoffs are that in these illustrations of the macro foundations of microeconomics, strong policy regimes suggest themselves. Our strategy can be also described as a constructive rendition of "analytic narratives" (Mongin, 2017). The task is to explain historical epochs with game theory tools. The agenda is riven by enthusiasts (economists and game theorists) and historians who are indifferent. Our formulations turn out be the least tendentious in dealing with two-player games and objective functions drawn from basic microeconomics. Uncertainty about the characteristics of systems is captured by differential equations working, to some extent, behind the backs of agents. Complexity is handled by different dynamical equations emanating from the same set of national income identities. Chapter 7 provides further proofs including an open-economy example.

Chapter 2

From Main Street to Wall Street

We trace the treatment of the topic through time. The start will be familiar to students of economic thought in the deep pondering over physical/real national production identities. However, the leading lights of economic science were not blind to the potentially debilitating role finance could play and the subject enters, appropriately, in a modern Marxian model. In our times, the full-blown intersection of Wall Street with Main Street is, of course, the work of Hyman Minsky.

2.1 From François Quesnay ...

The author of the *Tableau Économique*, 1759, figures in an introduction to the fraternity of models of which the SFC framework is a part. He is the guiding light illuminating the circuit approach to monetary macroeconomics. Like SFC models, the logic is structural and closed. In the model of Augusto Graziani, for instance, "initial finance" is the creation of money when a bank intermediates between business and labour and originates a process of production and "final finance" is associated with the expenditure of incomes arising thereby and the reflux of the wage outlay to firms in the form of profits. Firms repay their loans to banks closing the circuit (Fontana & Realfonzo, 2017). The special contribution of the French theorist in contrast to the input-output tables of the icons of classical political economy is the meld of technological coefficients and nominal values. The framework is not constructed in independent real and monetary terms. The nominal values that will drive our models are the product of prices and quantities.

Secondly, Quesnay's *Tableau* was not alone in being shot through with political economy. National Income Accounting has always been contested terrain. One description of the discipline is policy-based evidence (Assa, 2016). William Petty used his estimates to prove that taxes and "Publick Levies" would increase the wealth of the commonwealth. At the same time, the then British Prime Minister excluded labour income in his accounts because he wished to exclude the working class in the first proposal for a general income tax in Britain in 1798. In 1799 and 1802, Benjamin Bell prepared his estimates to challenge Pitt's numbers as well as argue for a repeal of the Corn Laws. The French Physiocrats, of whom Quesnay's *Tableau*

Économique was the most illustrious manifesto, were the prime movers in using economic theory to inform National Income computations.

For our purposes, we retain the emphasis on classes in the *Tableau* and the distinction between "productive expenditures" and "sterile expenses". Given the time of writing, the former was associated with agriculture. The latter included "interest on money" and "commercial expenses". Quesnay worried over the consumption of "luxuries" overtaking reproductive expenditures over time.

Another member of the pantheon that inspires circuitistes and SFC modelers alike is Joseph A Schumpeter. Schumpeter is always hard to identify in one's corner for his work best embodies the difficulty of moving from an evenly rotating economy adequately described by the tools of the theory of value to a rupture of that general equilibrium by new ways and means of producing goods and services spearheaded by the heroic entrepreneur. 'Schumpeterians' of different stripes have been developing models of technical change not requiring money, deriving sustenance from the master's seminal writings. A private enterprise economy is assumed wherein there is freedom to enter explicit and implicit contracts. The individual is the constitutive unit of the capitalist system. The theory of ophelimity (Vilfredo Pareto) is the proof that preferences and constraints determine all aggregate phenomena. To the standard theorems about substitutes and complements we would, today, add extensions in strategic complements and substitutes. The grand achievement of Léon Walras was the derivation of the conditions of general equilibrium. The system of exchange relationships renews itself from period to period. Sellers of commodities reappear as buyers with the wherewithal to purchase the commodities which would maintain their consumption and capital intact in the subsequent period at the current level and so on. Jean-Baptiste Say joins hands with Walras. The economy is dynamic in this sense. Each period is the basis of the next in that it generates data that enable workers and capitalists to repeat the same process in the next time interval. The economic system is, thus, stable. The capitalist dynamic can be extended to incorporate money. As with intermediate goods, there is no need to construct an independent exchange value of money as it is no more than a temporary abode of purchasing power as is an input. The value of money is derived from the value of consumption goods it commands. Walras' analysis is carried out for the case of a given stock of fiat money. Money is the $n + 1^{st}$ item in the initial endowment of households and firms. It has a price by virtue of its marginal utility function. The price, emerging in a market called the capital market, equates the demand for money with the available stock. At the hands of Kenneth Arrow and Gerard Debreu later, the future was envisioned as a tree with spreading branches with transactions at nodes across different states of the world and time points assumed possible. The foundations of finance were laid. The bases for hedging, futures, and options, and the hothouse outgrowths to follow will be found in Arrow securities.

Banking plays no role in the "circular flow". "Development", on the other hand, is the generation of surprises from within the "industrial and commercial" life of the economy. Schumpeter, it is well known, laid stress on the institution of "new combinations" by means of the creation of purchasing power by banks. All the same, the annual growth of savings which is the resultant of previous "development" is no less important. There are upper bounds to the possibility of financing entrepreneurs with no prior savings. Schumpeter examines the case of a gold standard and the institution of central banking. New commodities financed by the creation of fresh purchasing power will flow after a time lag. In the short run, prices will rise and the value of gold contained in the gold coin will exceed the value of the monetary unit. Bank IOUs will be presented for redemption. The solvency of banks will be threatened. If, in addition, there are constraints to the commodity complement of the freshly-minted notes coming to the market on time, banks must intervene with the savings of depositors. Thus, reserves are important both for commercial banks as well as central banks.

2.2 ... through Karl Marx ...

The circular production economy, most elegantly displayed by Piero Sraffa, demonstrates that production is a social process in which the production of commodities is technically connected through coefficients of production as well as socially connected through the corresponding activity of households, business enterprises, the State. Capitalists engage in the production of commodities with the expectation of earning a flow of money profits. Marx, Keynes, and others like Veblen, were joined in the perspective that the capitalist economy was a monetary production economy (Ho, 2016). The appropriation of money, $C' - M'$, in Marx's circuit of money capital is achieved through the conversion of working capital into inputs, $M - C$, required in the production process. Class conflict arises because of the tension between the reproduction of the working class or the enjoyment of use values $C - M - C'$ and the surplus maximization of the capitalist class $M - C - M'$.

Before we follow with a literal historical sequence, following Quesnay with the epoch-marker whose name adorns the title of this section, since we have broken off with Schumpeter to develop a thematic line, it is worth our while to detour through the work of Michal Kalecki, the Polish Marxist, a contemporary of Keynes who arrived at the results of the latter through a direct, less-complex route (Kalecki, 1943, 1953, 1971). Consider the determination of profits in a simple model without government. Gross National Product is the sum of gross investment and consumption. According to the other well known breakup, the value of GNP will be divided between workers and capitalists. The income of workers is wages and salaries, that of capitalists gross profits including depreciation and undistributed profits, dividends, rent and interest. Then

GNP	GNP
Gross Profits	Gross Investment
Wages and Salaries	Capitalists' Consumption
	Workers' Consumption

Kalecki makes the simplifying assumption that workers' consumption equals their income. In that case, Gross Profits = Gross Investment and Consumption of Capitalists. Of these components, capitalists may increase their consumption or their investment outlays above their present income. If the animal spirits of entrepreneurs are suddenly tickled, for instance, their investment activity will expand.

We record our first exposure to a theorem in the aggregate not deriving from individual demand and supply functions. The demand for construction materials, equipment and other intermediate goods does not come from an equivalent decrease in capitalist consumption. A purchase executive will activate the credit line of her company with its bank and in the effecting of the plans increase, through orders, by the same amount, the profits of other companies. While this overdraft facility is being activated, the credit of others is increasing. Aggregate production will increase to the point where profits derived from it is equal to consumption and investment. Capitalists cannot decide to increase their earnings. Their consumption and investment plans determine profits, not the other way around.

Kalecki derives the theorem, alternatively, in a less Keynesian, more Marxian manner. The system is composed of three Departments: a Department producing investment goods, a Department producing capitalists' consumption goods, and a Department producing workers' consumer goods or Basics. The last is the sum of wage goods consumed by the workers who produce them and wage goods consumed by the workers in the other two Departments. This surplus is the profit accruing to capitalists in the wage goods Department. If employment and wages in the first two Departments increase, the production of or drawing down of inventories of wage goods in the third Department will go up till the profit in Department III equals the increase in wages in Departments I and II. The production of Departments I and II will also determine the production of Department III, given a distribution between profits and wages in all Departments. The degree of monopoly plays a role in the theory of profits. Given the theorem, it is workers' income, here equal to workers' consumption, which is determined by the price markup. In summary form, capitalists' consumption and investment along with the degree of monopoly determine the consumption of workers and, thereby, aggregate output and employment.

Another Keynes-Kalecki tough research problem concerns the connection between the rate of interest and the rate of profit (Green, 1992; Pivetti, 1991). Here, connections with the framework of David Ricardo are sought. In the work of Ricardo the rate of interest and the rate of profit go hand in glove. The focus is on long-period equilibrium. The rate of interest is determined by the so-called real forces of productivity and thrift. It is equal to its natural value which is determined by the same forces that determine the rate of profit on the capital invested in enterprise. Marx wrestled with the problem about how this equality might come about. He drew upon the available evidence to question the Currency School doctrine that the rate of interest equalised the demand for and the supply of real capital. He argued that the notion of a natural rate of interest is slippery and the only number that matters is the market rate or indeed the spectrum of rates for commercial paper. This rate, in turn, depends upon the degree of monopoly in the banking sector. Marx and Keynes are joined in their rejection of the theorem that the rate of interest and the rate of profit converge. Keynesian elements can be gleaned in *Capital* in the form of the criticality of capitalists' impulses to a fresh commitment of idle hoards at a particular point of time as well as a 'speculative motive' theory of the interest rate. From Marx's numerous notes it can be inferred that the forces of competition include the search and assisting activity of banks. In a first glimpse of the principle of arbitrage, Marx noted that the banking sector, like other sectors of the economy, had to earn not less than the general rate of profit on wages and capital in order to fire the banking business.

We develop a contemporary treatment of the theme around MV Passarella, 2016, who, in turn, builds upon Marx's schemes of creation, circulation, and destruction of the monetary surplus of a manufacturing-based capitalist economy. Passarella endorses the modern writing of Marx's schemes of expanded reproduction in the form of difference equations. He advises connections with Post Keynesian and circuitist approaches for the development of the model. Furthermore, we endorse the suggestion to view the economy as moving non-ergodically from period to period.

2.2.1 The complexity of simple reproduction

The notations and treatment follow Passarella. Our economy is constituted by two Departments, Department I producing capital or investment goods subscripted by i and Department II producing consumer goods subscripted by c. Each process is assumed to take a fraction $1/n_j$ ($j = i,c$) of the period where n_j is a parameter representing the jth intra-period turnover rate. The depreciation rate is unity. That is, only circulating capital is employed. We turn to the monetary circuit for the origination of the process of production. Echoing "initial finance", commercial banks support the activity of firms by providing overdraft facilities for their wage bill. Denoting the average wage by w and the number of workers employed by L, distinguishing between sectors, the wage bills are w_jL_j, $j = i,c$. From a bank balance-sheet angle and by the precept of double-entry bookkeeping, the corresponding accounts of workers are a liability. Even in the textbook definition, deposits are money. Marx distinguished this variable capital V from constant capital C. In flow terms, in the current period we have $\Delta(w_jL_j) = \Delta(V_j)$, $j = i,c$. Now, denoting by S_j the surplus value created in the jth Department, by θ_j the sectoral retention rate of capitalists, and by $q_j = C_j/V_j$ the sectoral organic composition of capital, (OCC), $j = i,c$, our first two definitional relationships are Passarella's equations (1) and (2).

$$V_i = V_{i,-1} + \frac{S_{i,-1}.\theta_i}{1+q_i} \quad 1$$

$$V_c = V_{c,-1} + \frac{S_{c,-1}.\theta_c}{1+q_c} \quad 2$$

Denoting by $\varepsilon_j = S_j/V_j$ the rate of surplus value or the rate of exploitation of workers in the jth sector, we can write down Passarella's equations (5) and (6) in lagged form,

$$S_{i,-1} = V_{i,-1}.\, \varepsilon_{i,-1}.\, n_{i,-1} \quad 3$$

$$S_{c,-1} = V_{c,-1}.\, \varepsilon_{c,-1}.\, n_{c,,-1} \quad 4$$

Plugging 3 and 4 into 1 and 2, we get the difference equations we seek.

$$V_i = \left(1 + \frac{\theta_i.\varepsilon_{i,-1}.n_{i,-1}}{1+q_i}\right) V_{i,-1} \quad 5$$

$$V_c = \left(1 + \frac{\theta_c.\varepsilon_{c,-1}.n_{c,-1}}{1+q_c}\right) V_{c,-1} \qquad 6$$

Now, capitalists can consume the non-ploughed-back portion of the surplus or save it. Denoting by σ_j the marginal propensity to save of the capitalist in the *j*th sector, capitalists' unproductive expenditures in both Departments are

$$F_i = (1 - \theta_i).S_i.(1 - \sigma_i) \qquad 7$$

$$F_c = (1 - \theta_c).S_c.(1 - \sigma_c) \qquad 8$$

Our equations 7 and 8 depart from the parallel (7) and (8) in Passarella in that we do not introduce a wealth term. The stock of wealth in the 'present' is the accumulation of 'past' flows of surplus that are neither reinvested nor consumed. A final pair of definitions for this section are sectoral profit rates. We have

$$r_i = \frac{\theta_i.S_i+F_i}{V_i+C_i} \qquad 9$$

$$r_c = \frac{\theta_c.S_c+F_c}{V_c+C_c} \qquad 10$$

We lag these definitions and the motive is far from mechanical. The difference between the rates of profit in the 'present' and the 'past' opens a door to the debate around the falling rate of profit. We substitute the definitions of unproductive expenditures in 7 and 8 into 9 and 10 and, after simplification, we derive the following difference equations

$$\left(\frac{S_i}{V_i}\right) = \frac{(1+q_i).r_i}{(1+q_{i,-1}).r_{i,-1}} \left(\frac{S_{i,-1}}{V_{i,-1}}\right) \qquad 11$$

$$\left(\frac{S_c}{V_c}\right) = \frac{(1+q_c).r_c}{(1+q_{c,-1}).r_{c,-1}} \left(\frac{S_{c,-1}}{V_{c,-1}}\right) \qquad 12$$

Since the coefficients of both equations are products of two variables, it is not clear, mathematically at least, whether they are increasing or decreasing. Let us take the traditional case of a falling rate of profit across both Departments and a falling organic composition of capital in both as well. Let us call both coefficients $a_i(t)$. Then,

$a_i(t) \leq 1$. If k is any real number, $\frac{S_i}{V_i} = ke^{a_i(t)}$ is the solution of the equation. We can go on to specify an initial condition and, thereby, completely determine the value of k. In this case, $lim_{t\to\infty} ke^{a(t)} = k$. In that case, the initial condition is a sink where nearby solutions tend to it. When $k = 0$, the equilibrium point is the constant solution, $\frac{S_i}{V_i} = 0$. In that case, $lim_{t\to\infty} ke^{a(t)}$ equals ∞ when $k > 0$ and equals $-\infty$ when $k < 0$. In short, we have a bifurcation when the coefficients change from increasing to decreasing or vice versa.

2.2.2 A financial circuit instead of expanded reproduction

In the "final finance" stage of the monetary circuit, industrial capitalists approach investment banks to support their investment plans. However, capitalists can use the surplus above to accumulate financial assets, ΔF_j, with $j = i,c$. In an accounting framework, this increase in assets will cancel out with the increase in liabilities for the capitalist class as a whole (Passarella, 2016, p 15). Thus,

$$S_j - F_j - C_j = \Delta F_j \qquad 13$$

A straight use of our definitions and equations 3 (4) and 7 (8) simplifies the left-hand side to

$$\frac{F_j}{(1-\theta_j)(1-\sigma_j)}\left[1-(1-\theta_j)(1-\sigma_j)-\varepsilon_j.n_j\right] = \Delta F_j$$

In difference equation form, we have

$$F_j = \left[\frac{1}{(1-\theta_j)(1-\sigma_j)} - \frac{\varepsilon_j.n_j}{(1-\theta_j)(1-\sigma_j)}\right] F_{j,-1} \qquad 14$$

In this case, when $\varepsilon_j . n_j = 1$, the slightest change in the equation leads to a sharp change in the behaviour of the solutions. We have a bifurcation at this point. Financial assets represent claims to a portion of surplus value in the future (Cauwels & Sornette, 2012). If the right is not exercised, asset prices can display bubbly growth. However, as soon as the options are called, the law of value comes into force. Prices must correspond to a fundamental value. It is not possible to distribute more wealth than is produced.

2.3 ... to Godley-Cripps-Lavoie

It is necessary to establish the Old Keynesian (Godley-Cripps) and Post Keynesian (Godley-Lavoie) foundations of the discussion below. The philosophical building blocks of both edifices are Keynes' path-breaking contributions in his *Theory of Probability*. There are so-called facts to start with but for theorists as well as "practical men" there are "beliefs" about those facts as well as "confidence" held in those beliefs. Later, Minsky was to sew these concepts together into the dynamics of the real-financial cycle. The point at stake here is not the calculations of an individual consumer or saver but categories that emerge and evolve through the rhythms of the capitalist cycle. Optimism and pessimism over the business climate is uninteresting, even if meaningful, if calculated as an index for a set of businessmen only.

Thus, the interest rate is not pivotal in determining investment. Profit expectations play that role. Working through the multiplier, the scale of operations will keep rising either because of windfall gains or as the proceeds of the sale of stocks is expended. Banks' loans to capitalists, in the case of a shortage of savings, are repaid only partially. As the sequence unfolds, banks will have to inject liquidity to be added to the revolving fund of finance in order to finance a steady rate of investment. This new money will be created in a progressively decreasing measure as the multiplier works itself out. Also, savings and liquidity cannot be conceptualised separately. The pressure on the liquidity position of banks during the unfolding of the multiplier can be ascribed to increasing activity as well as a shortage of saving. In sympathy with Dennis Robertson in his debate with Keynes, as with the nuanced reading of Schumpeter earlier, both processes are equivalent, one from the point of view of loanable funds, the other from the perspective of liquidity preference. The theory of liquidity preference must include a direct link from savings supply to the rate of interest. The problem to be addressed is that of the ability of the banking system and the holders of speculative balances to counteract the effects on interest rates which arise from a shortage of savings and a dearth of liquidity that occur as the economy transits towards a new equilibrium with a higher level of expenditure. The monetary determination of the rate of interest needs the computation of the liquidity preference of banks (Green, 1992). The supply of credit depends on the degree of aversion of banks to lending. A fall in bank liquidity preference would lead to a rise in bank assets and liabilities as well as a change in the composition of assets.

No better way to illustrate all of the above than through a description of Minsky's framework. A fruitful transition from the short-run dynamics of a macroeconomic model and the real-financial fluctuations associated with Minsky would be the probe of a benchmark macroeconomic model offered by him (Minsky, 1986)

$$Y = C + I$$

$$C = C(Y)$$

$$I = I(P_{IS}, \overline{W})$$

$$P_K = L(M, \overline{K})$$

$$P_{ID} = P_K$$

$$P_{IS} = P_{ID}$$

$$M_D = M_S$$

The model is not unfamiliar from introductory macroeconomics where the exogenous variable M is money, and the subscripts D and S against it denote demand for and supply of money in the money market equilibrium condition. $\overline{K}$ and $\overline{W}$ are the given capital stock and wage bill respectively and the 'price' of money $P_M = 1$. P_{IS} is the supply price of a unit of investment, P_K is the market price of existing real capital, and P_{ID} is the demand price of a unit of investment.

The explanatory sequence is as follows: The portfolio balance equation or the liquidity preference relation above yields a value of P_K for every quantity of M. Given W, I adjusts so that $P_{IS} = P_K$. Once I is given, C and Y are determined. However, productivity of capital takes the form of expected future earnings (gross profits after taxes) of an assembly of capital goods within a producing unit. Recall the arithmetical relation that the value of the capital stock will necessarily equal the discounted value of a stream of returns. The MEC can be substituted for the equation for P_K. Hence, this is the unstable equation in the system and shifts downwards whenever a wave of pessimism overcomes investors. Changes in investors' confidence can lead to potentially destabilising macroeconomic cycles even when the interest rate is relatively stable in the face of aggregate demand shocks. Building upon Keynes, Minsky argued that the explanation for the level of aggregate demand must be sought in the financial markets, in the financing of investment plans. Disequilibria therein affect the valuation of capital assets relative to the price of current output and this price ratio determines investment activity. Keynes' *General Theory,* Minsky explained, was concerned with how these two sets of prices (capital and financial assets on the one hand and current output and wages on the other) were determined in different markets by different explanatory variables which gave rise to fluctuations in economic activity.

Minsky's cycle moves through the following stages: "Hedge financing" best describes the tranquil period when the anticipated cash flows from operations are adequate to meet future commitments on debts. Over a few such years, confidence and optimism build to generate "speculative financing" wherein the present value of cash flows over a finite horizon are not expected to meet payments commitments. As a run of good years continues, "Ponzi financing" schemes are generated which are outright pyramidal swindles where a subclass of individuals roll over their debt by emitting fresh debt in a never-ending spiral. It is worth observing as a footnote here that the standard infinite-horizon optimisation exercise in advanced texts includes the well-known "No Ponzi Games condition" that excludes these schemes on the grounds of the rationality of borrowers and lenders. At the euphoric peak of the cycle as both short-term and long-term interest rates drive speculative and Ponzi behaviour, the present values of some Ponzi-type investors will turn negative. Reneging on their commitments will lead to the distress of their lenders who will encash other financial assets. The prices of assets across the board will plummet precipitously impacting on investment plans and profits. While the upper point of the cycle, then, is characterised by a Keynes-type evaporation of euphoria, the lower turning point is a process of debt deflation leading to a stable system with modest hedge funding of projects. We provide a formal treatment of the Minsky scheme in Section 6.3.2.

We return to the main course with the seminal profit equation of Godley-Cripps, 1983, (hereafter G&C, A9.1, p 186)

$$\Pi = FE + \Delta I - WB - T - R.I_{-1} \qquad 15$$

where Π is profits, *FE* is the value of final sales (just private sector purchases *PE* if a closed economy without government or $PE + G$ where G is government expenditure), ΔI is the change in the value of inventories in the accounting period ($\Delta I = I - I_{-1}$, the difference between the end period and beginning period value of inventories), *WB* is the total wage bill, T is sales tax net of subsidies, and R is the rate of interest. As an illustration of the connection between stocks and flows, present policy and the interval just past, we use the following SFC norms (G&C, p 187). For the purpose, we have the definition of "historical costs" $HC \equiv WB - \Delta I$. First, we have the proportion of historic costs of sales in each period carried over from earlier periods, (A9.3)

$$\kappa \equiv I_{-1} / HC \qquad 16$$

The profit mark up on total costs is (A9.4)

$$\lambda \equiv \Pi / (HC + R.I_{-1}) \qquad 17$$

Finally, an average sales tax rate is defined in the following manner, (A9.5)

$$\tau \equiv T / (HC + R.I_{-1} + \Pi) \qquad 18$$

It is a trivial matter to combine these definitions to derive an equation connecting the sales tax, a policy variable with the profit markup.

$$T \equiv (1 + \lambda)[I_{-1} + \kappa(R.I_{-1})] / \kappa \qquad 19$$

At this level of aggregation, it is not possible to finesse the sales tax as falling on Non Basics as against Basics. Kalecki concluded as much from his model. Here, we have a connection between the sales tax and the degree of monopoly, λ. G&C bring inflation into the picture in Fisher equation-like terms with $(1 + R) = (1 + r)(1 + \%p)$ where r is the real rate of interest and $\%p$ is the rate of inflation (G&C, pp 187, 192). In words, 'lower' indirect taxes supplement the wage bill increasing in lockstep with productivity increases to keep the inflation rate rising in correspondence.

In another translation, we have the Kaleckian equation (Tymoigne, 2008)

$$\Pi = I - S_W + DEF + NX \qquad 20$$

where Π is gross profits after taxes, S_W is the savings of the working class, I is gross private domestic investment, *DEF* the fiscal deficit of the government, and *NX* net exports. There is a positive feedback loop in the equation running from profits to investment. Profits are sustained by investment which, in turn, is sustained by investment plans. Through its fiscal stance, the government can mute this destabilizing loop. All it needs do is put, say, green projects in the communal pot and let the private sector pick and choose. The government would signal, thereby, the areas in which investment is to flow without undertaking the business itself nor taking ownership of these 'commanding heights'. Non Basics production would be left to the private sector while housing, roads, and so on would be orchestrated by the government. The vicious spiral implicit in the above equation would, thereby, be eliminated.

The innovation associated with methodologies close to Keynes like the SFC framework and Kalecki is to begin with the postulate that a generalised price-setting market structure is an adequate characterisation of a modern economy. Therefore, the price of the product of an industry is the outcome of firms imposing a mark-up on average prime costs which is assumed to be approximately constant up to full capacity. The mark-up, synonymous with the degree of monopoly of the industry, determines the profit margin and the share of profits in aggregate income. The level of profits is determined by the level of investment that entrepreneurs implement. In other words, pricing and investment behaviour determine the level of employment and output. The mark-up rate is believed to be relatively insensitive to the state of demand. Fluctuations in economic activity flow mainly from fluctuations in investment expenditures.

Thus, consider the Kaleckian Departmental schema of Section 2.1.1. Suppose that in a certain period, the annual wage bill increases as result of increasing wage rates. Denote the pre-change wage bills in the first two Departments by w_{I} and w_{II} and the fraction by which wages change by α. The increment in the wage bill in the first two Departments, then, is $\alpha(w_{\mathrm{I}} + w_{\mathrm{II}})$. Profits in these Departments decline arithmetically. The increment in the wage bill of these Departments, though, implies a rise in profits of Department III by the identical amount. Either output (excess capacity) or prices or both will rise there. Total profits remain the same. The prices of investment goods and capitalist consumption goods will rise as a result of the wage hike. The volume of capitalist investment and consumption is unaltered in the short run. In other words, profits in the first two Departments rise by $1+\alpha$. The production and consumption of wage goods remain the same. Thus, profits in the third Department also rise by $1+\alpha$. Thus the volume of production in all three Departments remains constant while the value in each increases by $1+\alpha$.

Higher markups will encourage trade unions to bargain with their employers for higher wages since the degree of monopoly is indeterminate and firms can charge lower prices. If their demands are granted but oligopolistic structures remain unaltered prices will also increase. A fresh round of demands for higher wages is the result and a price-wage spiral is underway. However, there is an upper bound to consumer prices. Trade union power restrains the unbridled rise of markups. Indeed, if the working class is organized and powerful, a redistribution of National Income from profits to wages could take place. In our illustration, profits in Department III increase in the same proportion as wage rates. However, if there is a redistribution as a result of the reduction in markups there, the wage bill in the third Department increases more than the wage rates. There is a rise in output and employment there but not in the first two Departments.

A word here on the distinction between money and real wages. An increase in aggregate output is associated, given the level of wages and costs of raw materials, with an increase in marginal costs which must be met by a proportionate rise in prices. However, higher prices of finished goods and given wage rates imply a fall in real wages which accompanies this expansion of output. Furthermore, with an increase in production the demand for intermediate goods will also go up. The prices of finished goods will rise for this additional reason reducing real wages further. An increase in production can also result from a decline in real wages as the result of a cut in money wages, prices of final goods remaining constant. The marginal costs of the goods at the initial level of output will fall inducing firms to expand output to the point where marginal cost equals price. Under imperfect competition, we know the price-marginal cost equality condition does not hold. A reduction in wages might tend to widen the divergence because some prices will be relatively rigid and not decline in the same proportion as wages. Consequently, as the money wages of workers initially decrease, their real purchasing power will decline proportionately to the fall in their wages. The demand for wage goods will fall and, with it, a fall in employment in the output of Department III. Consequently, the decline in real wages due to prices being more sticky than wages is associated with a fall in employment.

We conclude this section with an account of Kalecki's political business cycle as an exemplification of an institutional story that backs the equations above. The context for most capitalist regimes is parliamentary democracy. In such a social economy, all government policy is in tune with the electoral process. The elections are the outcomes of business, working class, and other sectarian interests. The force of Kalecki's theory is the classes whose interests the extant government must keep before it in making policy choices. A government spending program could ensure full employment in a capitalist regime if there was sufficient unutilised capacity to employ the labour force. However, business would resist government intervention designed to deliver full employment. The opposition of government intervention by the capitalist class is not easy to understand at the level of macroeconomic identities. Profits, after all, rise with full employment. Additional government spending is unaccompanied by increased taxation. Yet, the threats of escalating working class strength and of potential inflation pressures loom large. Under a capitalist system, business holds the cards with government because private investment, and the level of employment it determines, depends on certainty equivalents of the future. Once the government establishes itself as an employer of last resort, it can be indifferent to the degree of confidence of investors. Looked at from a different angle, budget deficits are regarded as anathema. In contrast, the capitalist class is mute against policies that induce profit-making activity like protectionist tariffs, breaking the backs of trade unions, and so on. Election-determined cycles of around 4 to 5 years would emerge from a situation where the government would stimulate the economy only to withdraw as the upswing gained momentum waving the flag 'overheating' and then reenter when employment approached critical levels. Succinctly, there would be a government-generated Phillips curve. The politico-economic cycle turned out to be a small research agenda after Kalecki. He considered a party in opposition that has just come to power on the promise of cutting a wage-price spiral. Accordingly, the new party in power implements a deflationary package. The effects of the stance become slowly visible in the growing register of the unemployed. Resentment grows again after a few years and as the next election is around the corner defeat seems imminent. Policy goes into reverse gear. In sum, the stop-go cycle consists of two phases; too much too late as a result of doing too little too early. Coming to the present, not a few have characterized the dispensation in America, in particular, and large swathes of the world, in general, as the contemporary form of fascism. The term embodies the absence of conflict between the incumbent government and the party waiting in the wings and between shifting alliances with capital and labour. All parties and classes are wedded to financial interests.

Kalecki, like Keynes, prognosticated increasing government activity in areas traditionally earmarked for private enterprise. Initially, the government would confine itself, in the well known fashion, to areas like physical and social infrastructure that complemented private activities. The capitalist class would not be displeased because the ease of doing business was smoothened. However, businessmen would resist the creep of government intervention as the steps included the takeover or nationalisation of transport and public utilities and, perhaps, banks. To be precise, capitalists would welcome government support of consumption by means of family allowances, price subsidies for basics, children's allowances, and so on. The profit motive is unimpaired. However, a regime of permanent full employment would be staunchly resisted. For, the maturity and sophistication of the working class would grow. While it is true that with full employment profits rise, Kalecki believed that the capitalist class would rather take a cut in profits than face the prospect of increasing working class militancy. An additional reason has been referred to. A through-cycle commitment to full employment might entail a redistribution of income. Incomes policies like wage-price guidelines would, therefore, face vigorous counter action.

Is reducing the degree of uncertainty for businessmen enough to pull an economy out of a recession? Kalecki did not think so. While procyclical interest rate policies might shorten the duration and reduce the amplitude of the cycle, full employment will not be attained even in the boom for political reasons although the level of employment will fluctuate less. If the measure is repeated time after time, in a remarkable prescience, Kalecki envisaged a situation when the rate of interest turned negative and the corporate income tax was transformed into a subsidy. None of these have any bearing on the mood of businessmen being in the doldrums because their expectations of the future are clouded by the data of the present. During a recession that refuses to go away, investment plans would be indifferent to any fall in the interest rate. Tax reliefs would be ineffective as the large bodily shift in the investment schedule towards the origin exceeds by far any movement along the given curve. Consequently, it is perfectly consistent with encouraging private investment to undertake public investment as well. The situation is one of crowding in. Once more, the capitalist class would not counter public investment financed by borrowing. They would take up cudgels, though, against output generated by subsidising consumption and a regime of full employment.

We have concluded our survey of non micro-founded political economy germane to our theme. Borrowing and lending and the behaviour of banks were always within the horizon of the giants whose shoulders we stand on. Others have developed Kalecki's seminal "principle of increasing risk" in writing scripts of financial crises.

Chapter 3

Some macro foundations

We show that macro of the old classical-Keynesian lineage was sufficiently fecund to portray complex institutional variety. Terms in universally-accepted macroeconomic arithmetic will be moved this way and that to model economies all over the world still stuck in feudalism traps. The 20th century growth model positive-normative response would be the tracking of the movement from agriculture to industry. Theorists in the 21st century have tried to solve the puzzle of the transition from agriculture to services, bypassing manufacturing. We pose the following question in the next section to be answered later: What inhibits a policy-induced technological revolution in agriculture? The following section describes political economy dearest to everyone's hearts. We capture "financialization" mathematically and propose a monetary policy response all from "political arithmetick" (William Petty).

3.1 Institutional variety in the transition to capitalism

We display our research practice of working with a set of macroeconomic identities with a lag structure that arises from the definitions. Putting them together some categories are retained, others recede into the background, and a difference equation (or two) emerge(s). Classes that drive the aggregates come to the fore, others retire to the shadows to remerge when called upon by a subsection. In the first part of this present subsection we examine the dynamics of a country that, while possessed of an embryonic capitalist sector, has not fully transited from the political economy of agrarian relations. Accordingly, as many including Kalecki in his treatment of "intermediate regimes" has done, to the traditional two-fold typology we must add the ruling class in agriculture that is torn between rebirth as capitalist farmers in the making and landlords continuing to be umbilically tied to earning rents on land. Tenants can, accordingly, become workers on farms or remain tenants. In the case of the latter and small and marginal farmers, the only desperate option is migration to the cities to swell the ranks of the unemployed there.

Our theme is labour-using technical change in agriculture. We set up two growth regimes in the countryside in which it can occur. In the first, the interaction is between capitalists-entrepreneurs and workers-households. In the second, capitalists and entrepreneurs are in conflict. Our penchant for seeking foundations in the classics leads us to Richard Cantillon (Grieve, 2015). In the 1730s, Cantillon foresaw the non-unique path agrarian economies could take. Therefore, it was not possible to make commodity values commensurate in terms of heterogeneous land. The solution was to express relative values by money outlays by entrepreneurs to hire land (rents) and labour (wages). Rent and wages in turn are the resultant of a tussle between landlords and workers. Farmers must set sales prices as a markup over their rental costs. Since Cantillon was concerned with an agricultural economy, the rate of profit on capital did not figure as an analytical category. Our model can be regarded as an extension in that respect. We note, though, that Cantillon's interest stemmed from the theorem that the number of people that can be supported in a country depends on the quantity of land devoted to the production of Basics, food being the Basic par excellence. In this regard, modern Marxists offer "comparative political economy" which comprises the orthodox relations of production in the form of class conflict and productive forces (Byres, 2016). According to this appraisal, conditions for capitalist accumulation exist but depend upon the combination of class interests. A "strategic" path to agrarian capitalism can be laid either through a class of landlords or a class of agrarian capitalists. From a modern political economy perspective, so-called new developmentalism contributes a wedge between productive capitalists and their profits and rentier capitalists earning rents and capital gains (Bresser-Pereira, 2015, 2016). That is to say, developmental and liberal class coalitions can be distinguished. In the group of middle-income countries, the latter comprises of rentiers and financiers who manage their wealth. The former consists of business managers and workers. As a country makes the transition to mature capitalism, a redistribution of wealth occurs.

The components will be culled from but generalise the concepts in the Duncan Foley & Thomas Michl, 1999, (hereafter F&M) volume. The notations are as follows. With X being gross product in an economy in a period, $x = X/N$ where N is the number of workers employed in the economy is labour productivity, $\rho = X/K$ where K is the assembly of the capital stock in the period is the output-capital ratio, capital stock per worker $k = K/N$ is a measure of capital intensity. For the sake of convenience, we ignore depreciation of the capital stock. Since we consider production with land, $u = U/N$ is land per employed worker and $\sigma = X/U$ is the productivity of land. Cantillon, in the steps of William Petty, would introduce a "par" between land and labour. Following F&M, we take the amount of land required per unit of capital as the unit of land so that $u = k$. We assume that there are businessmen who organize production by renting land from landowners and capital from capitalists and employing workers. In the case of the first relationship, both parties will negotiate over rent on land, v_{ut}. The asset price of land p_{ut} in terms of output or capital must adjust so that all stocks of capital and land are held.

The no-arbitrage condition here means (F&M, p 205)

$$1 + v_{kt} = \frac{p_{ut+1} + v_{ut}}{p_{ut}} = 1 + g_{p_{ut}} + \frac{v_{ut}}{p_{ut}} \qquad 21$$

F&M use the symbol g_Y to denote the growth rate of a variable *Y*. In order to produce *X* units of output in a period, the businessman must hire $N = X/x$ workers. The wage bill is $W = wX/x$ where w is the average wage. The forces of competition result in the businessmen paying the residual revenue to the capitalists at the end of the period. The zero profit condition for the capitalist is (F&M, p 202)

$$v_{kt} + v_{ut} = \frac{1 - w_t}{k_t} \qquad 22$$

Combining Equations 21 and 22,

$$g_{p_{ut}} + \left(1 + \frac{1}{p_{ut}}\right) v_{ut} = \frac{1 - w_t}{k_t} \qquad 23$$

Assuming a population growth rate of n, the requirement of full employment (F&M, p 111) is

$$\frac{K_t}{k_t} = N_t \qquad 24$$

Full employment will be achieved in the next period if

$$N_{t+1} = (1 + n)N_t = (1 + n)\frac{K_t}{k_t} = \frac{K_{t+1}}{k_{t+1}} \qquad 25$$

Multiplying the left-hand side of equation 25 by the no-arbitrage conditions given in 23, we get

$$\left(\frac{1 - w_t}{k_t}\right) N_{t+1} = (1 + n)\left\{g_{p_{ut}} + \left(1 + \frac{1}{p_{ut}}\right) v_{ut}\right\} N_t \qquad 26$$

One difference equation of the system can be expressed as follows.

$$N_{t+1} = (1+n)\left(\frac{k_t}{1-w_t}\right)\left\{g_{p_{ut}} + \left(1+\frac{1}{p_{ut}}\right)v_{ut}\right\}N_t \qquad 27$$

We define land-saving technical change as the following positive growth rate,

$g_\sigma = \sigma_{+1}/\sigma - 1$ or $\sigma_t = \sigma_0(1 + \varphi)^t$. In that case, from our definitions, we can derive the following expression, $u_t = u_0(1 + \varphi)^t$, where $u_0 = x_0/\sigma$ is land intensity in the 'base year'. Referring to the right-hand side of Equation 25,

$$N_{t+1} = (1+n)N_t = (1+n)\frac{K_t}{k_t} = \frac{K_{t+1}}{(1+\varphi)k_t} \qquad 28$$

Equation 28 can be alternatively written as

$$K_{t+1} = (1+n)(1+\varphi)K_t \qquad 29$$

Our alternative ways of presenting the dynamics of our model, equations 27 and 29, serve to highlight a tension F&M (1999, p 291) observe in the model. The first equation underscores the importance of production. The wage rate is a cost which the entrepreneur will attempt to minimize. The conflict here is that between capitalists-entrepreneurs choosing $k(t)$ to maximize their payoffs in conflict with workers-households who chose $w(t)$ to maximize their (indirect) utility. The second equation depicts the accumulation of capital driven by technical change. This time a class of entrepreneurs who choose $\varphi(t)$ to maximize its inter temporal profits is at the forefront. Capitalists plan their investment (the accumulation of capital) to maximize their profits. The two might not be in conflict. The profits of the entrepreneur resulting from a change in the technological coefficients might be increased by an increase in the stock of capital. We provide further motivation, set up and solve this differential game in Section 6.1.

3.2 Institutional variety in advanced capitalism

We continue to combine and disassemble system-wide sets of identities and definitions, concluding with a difference equation or two. Once derived, we scrutinise the equations to identify the agents/classes pushing or pulling the economy. We see that pairs of protagonists emerge naturally. Other agents/classes recede into the background only because the aggregates defining them are not in current use. We present three historical-normative institutional configurations. The first is an economy in which banks are the "ephor" as Schumpeter would put it of the system; the second is a model in which a stock market is central to the allocation of credit in the economy; in the third, the long-term government bond is the monetary axis of private-sector choices.

The macroeconomic framework is drawn from Godley and Lavoie, 2007, (hereafter, G&L). Our first model is as follows. We begin with familiar macroeconomic identities,

$$C + I + G = Y = WN + F \qquad 30$$

where C is aggregate consumption, I is investment, G is public expenditure. The wage bill is the product of the money wage W and the number of individuals employed in the period under consideration N. The other item of income is profits F. Disposable income $YD = Y - T$. Taxes T are imposed on incomes, $T = \theta WN$. Savings $S = Y - T - C$. The simplest case is one in which households convert all their savings into bank deposits M. Government deficits $G - T$ are assumed to be supported by the issue of high-powered money H. That is, $\Delta H = G - T$. Governments could also could sell short-term bills B to the public and the central bank to finance its fiscal deficit. Ignoring the interest disbursal on government paper previously contracted for, usually considerable, the earlier equation would be $\Delta B = G - T$. In both instances, banks must compulsorily commit a portion of their deposits with the central bank as cash reserves (or bills). Call BLR this bank liquidity ratio. We assume, to simplify, that only banks hold base money (or bills), $H = BLR.M$. Another norm that impacts on banking systems the world over through Basel is the capital adequacy ratio $CAR = M/L$. Note that $CAR.BLR = H/L$. Finally, firms maintain credit lines with banks to support their inventory holdings IN. In other words, the accumulation of inventories implies fresh bank loans, $\Delta L = \Delta IN = I$ (we exclude amortization funds from our definition because they are relatively less important for our purposes). Ignoring own equity, the balance sheets of commercial banks is $H = M - L$. Banks are assumed committed by one-period contracts to provide a rate of return r^m on deposits as are earnings from loans to firms given by a one-period interest rate on loans r^l. As a reminder, G&L's notation for dynamics is $\Delta x \equiv x - x_{-1}$. All profits of firms are assumed to be distributed to households. Thus, the disposable income of households is $YD = WN + F - T + r^m_{-1}M_{-1}$. Also, $F = C + G - WN + \Delta IN - r^l_{-1}IN_{-1}$. Deducting T from the two versions of National Income in equation 30 and using the definitions above, we arrive at the following dynamic expression in loans. It could equivalently be expressed in terms of high-powered money.

$$(CAR.BLR)\Delta L = G - \theta WN - r_{-1}^{l} L_{-1}$$

In so-called state-space form, the equation is

$$L = \left(1 - \frac{r_{-1}^{l}}{CAR.BLR}\right) L_{-1} + \frac{G - \theta WN}{CAR.BLR} \qquad 31$$

The classic class conflict on display is that the worker makes her work choices $N(t)$ so as to maximize her utility and the business executive chooses her wage bill so as to minimize her costs. We defer reflections on the properties of the solution of the equation to Section 3.3.

The second configuration represents the primacy of financial markets summarized in the expression "financialization". G&L analyse a general form of investment behaviour with a portion of investment plans supported by retained profits and with relations with banks intact. In order to contrast this regime with the previous, we assume that investment plans are financed entirely by the issue of equity. That is $I = \Delta e p_e$, where e is the issue sold by firms and p_e is the price of equity. The stock-flow norm of concern here is the price earnings ratio $PE = p_e e_{-1}/F$. It could be regarded as a measure of "financialization". A high value of the ratio implies a high value of current equity and/or a low value of profits arising from the production of goods and services. Using these definitions in equation 30 we get

$$C + \Delta e p_e + G = WN + p_e e_{-1}/PE \qquad 32$$

The build up to this description indicates that it is the household representation of the representative agent that is called upon. The problem is converted to the problem of choosing $C(t)$ to maximize her utility. As with the first regime, further analysis of this equation is postponed to Sections 3.3 and 6.2.2.

In order to appreciate the third policy regime, we need to understand the origins of fiat money in the government bond. Thus, the Continental Dollar was a zero-interest bearer bond and not a fiat currency (Grubb, 2013). In 1775, Congress determined the quantity, nominal value, and redemption method for the first two emissions of the Continental Dollar. The policy was simple:

remit and burn. In the interest of perfect credibility, the government set future taxes to redeem and remove the paper money out of circulation. The New Jersey paper was a savings bond-type money where time discounting explained almost all its present value. It traded at less than its face value not because of depreciation but because it was a zero-interest bond and would not be redeemed at its face value until some time in the distant future. The instrument had been an object both of conflict and cooperation between the Federal Reserve and the Treasury (Humpage, 2014). During the Second World War, the Federal Reserve sacrificed monetary policy to the needs of the Treasury when it agreed to pay yield on Treasury securities. The Federal Reserve maintained a low and steep fixed yield curve. The low yields minimized the Treasury's borrowing costs. Investors were convinced of the futility of awaiting higher yields and there was no risk of capital losses in holding long-term securities. Thus, long-term securities were almost as liquid as short-term securities. A century ago, Keynes in the *Treatise* made the case that central banks could reverse recessions directly by actively trading in bond markets (Turner, 2011). Later, many of those who gave testimony before the hearings that culminated in the Radcliffe Committee Report argued that the main effect of monetary policy on aggregate demand was through the long-term rate of interest. Assume then, bond and only bond financing of the deficit. BL is long-term bonds and p_{bL} their price. The bonds are consols, pieces of paper which pay the owner one unit of fiat money, the coupon per period forever. In other words, if there are BL_{-1} bonds in existence, the interest disbursed on the stock is BL_{-1}. Ignoring this term on the right-hand side, we have $\Delta BLp_{bL} = G - T$. Comparing this expression with similar equations above, only the left-hand side is changed with bonds replacing base money or bills. Now assume for tractability that only households hold government bonds. One consequence is that capital gains on these bond holdings must be added to the disposable income of households YD in what is known as Haig-Simons income, $YD_{HS} = YD + \Delta p_{bL}BL$. G&L set great store by the following breakup of the change in the value of bonds. Indeed, a Danish student who provided the proof was rewarded with a bottle of whisky by Professor Godley (G&L, p 135)! In difference terms, the change in the value of bonds is $\Delta BL\Delta p_{bL} = \Delta BLp_{bL} + BL\Delta p_{bL}$. A third breakup of national income can be added to the two of equation 30. That is, $Y = YD + T$. Putting the equations in this section together, we get

$$\Delta BL\Delta p_{bL} = YD_{HS} - C - I \quad (33)$$

There is a basic difference with the earlier two state equations in that investment appears for the first time. It might seem strange that the foundation stone of Post Keynesian macroeconomics has not entered the construction of the structure till the finishing touches of a public policy regime. However, Keynes' theory is a regarded as financial theory of investment as part of a theory of cycles (Kregel, 2014). Indeed, one institutional setup suggested as an ameliorative device is the installation of a permanent government investment bank along the lines of the Reconstruction Finance Corporation. In keeping with the instructions following the two equations above, the stability of the equation is the subject of the next section.

3.3 Stabilizing Stock-Flow Norms

We consider the stability properties of the G&L difference equations derived above. Our first equation 31 is reproduced below.

$$L = \left(1 - \frac{r_{-1}^{l}}{CAR.BLR}\right)L_{-1} + \frac{G - \theta WN}{CAR.BLR}$$

The dynamics of the system depends upon the combination of *CAR* and *BLR* alongside the rate of interest on loans contracted between banks and businessmen as well as the budget deficit. In the aftermath of the financial crisis in the US in 2008, central banks the world over became painfully aware of the porous checks and balances in place to curb the proliferation of instruments and activities of the Wall Street conglomerates. Secondly, liquidity dries up in the aftermath of all financial crises. The provision of adequate and timely liquidity is the main chapter of various scripts for banking being written across the world. That great sage of modern monetary economics, Charles Goodhart, 2017, has summarised the state of play post-2007 pithily in three myths held pre-2007. The first is that only capital adequacy norms from Basel will solve problems of solvency, the second is that liquidity is always available in wholesale markets, and the third that maturity mismatches in the banking system can be ignored at nobody's peril.

The equilibrium solution of the non-homogenous equation is

$$L = \frac{G - \theta WN}{r_{-1}^{l}}$$

A 'low' interest rate goes with a high level of lending in equilibrium. However, scholars have drawn attention to the link between the zero interest rate bound and financial disintermediation (McKinnon, 2014). The sluggish recovery of developed countries from the crisis in 2008 is connected with a lacklustre growth in bank credit to SMEs. SMEs have been the engine of employment in previous recoveries. On the other hand, direct finance to large corporates recovered rapidly. Markets for stocks and bonds and commercial paper were buoyant soon after 2008 resulting in numerous IPOs and mergers and acquisitions. As short-term interest rates get lower, larger corporate borrowers find it profitable to raise resources by selling short-term commercial paper to other corporates and money-market mutual funds for less than the prime loan rate of banks. Smaller banks, those with a riskier portfolio of loans to SMEs, are caught out with the need to raise more bank capital to support their informationally-opaque and thus costlier loans. Consequently, they call in or reject applications to renew loans or shy away from fresh lending. On the other hand, the crowding-in of bank lending by government expenditure is relatively unambiguous. All three components specified in the solution are important; the quality of government expenditure, the income tax rate and the wage bill which, in turn, is the product of the average wage and the number of people employed. We flesh out and provide the solutions to the optimization problems of the characters behind the aggregates that emerge in Section 6.2.1.

Equation 32 is a characterisation of "financialization" also reproduced.

$$C + \Delta e p_e + G = WN + p_e e_{-1} / PE$$

The requirement for stability deduced later is $\left(1 + \frac{1}{PE}\right) < 1$. The negative requirement of PE is the stability expectation of "financialization". Either profits in manufacturing and so on must be non positive and/or one or other stock market index must be negative. Recent American history supports the former conjecture.

In the final instance of the equivalence of the government bond and money, we have equation 33,

$$\Delta BL \Delta p_{bL} = YD_{HS} - C - I$$

In this case when fiat money is defined as the government bond which 'self-destructs' and mirrors real activity, there is no need for SFC norms or the specification of stability corridors. In the steady state of the equation above when $G = T$ the basic macroeconomic identity $YD = C + I$ is restored.

Chapter 4

The trip back to Main Street from Wall Street

Moving far enough down Wall Street, the return to Main Street is rocky and unilluminated. We critically survey the well-known guidelines which essentially recommend erecting barriers between the two, between virtuous and the vicious, within the purview of our modeling language. The first two sections below construct the roadblocks for developed economies, the latter two for developing economies.

4.1 Financialization

The financialization of GDP has negative effects on the aggregate from an instrumental point of view in its divergence from employment trends. Metrics like the debt-GDP ratio are used inappropriately to evaluate growth trajectories. Above all, the measurement of profits is of essential importance. G&L distinguish between the conceptual category of entrepreneurial profits and the recorded profits of corporations which include financial fees which are only transfers. With the System of National Accounts (SNA) 1993 fees from financial services began to be counted as productive activity. The fact remains that the revenues associated with these services represent an opportunity cost for households and firms since the money spent could have been used in productive activities. Along the negative correlation between finance's share in output and employment, the suggestion is that the sector is extractive rather than productive, value reducing rather than value enhancing. Differently put, the value added by finance should be deducted not excluded from GDP. The reason is that it is the modern intermediate cost not an intermediate input to intermediate consumption to all industries producing use value.

Ben Fine et al, 2016, work out the link between money and commodities. Despite the variety of commodities, all money-commodity relations share common elements by virtue of representing exchange value. Since finance is of a higher order on the same base, it too is associated with money and commodities. It is only in the current epoch, 1974 - 2016, that return of equity

(ROE) has emerged as the norm of so-called shareholder value capitalism. The transformation of the business of making commercial loans was driven by the pressure of borrowers to secure lower lending rates and the rising costs incurred by banks to screen and monitor the applicants. On the other side, deposit taking evolved into a high-cost activity that resisted increases in productivity. Asset securitization provided the means for firms to obtain liquid funding cheap for both their short-term and long-term requirements. The first step in the process was the issue of commercial paper as a substitute for bank lending. At any point of time, banks must take decisions on the allocation of credit. Incentives may be such as to induce them to lend against existing assets rather than lend for investment in productive activities (Ryan Collins et al, 2016). The following notations are drawn from G&L. Let e_b denote the stock of equities supplied by banks and p_b their price. As earlier, the stock of equities supplied by firms is e_f and their price p_f. Thus, balance sheets take on a life with $\Delta e_i p_i$, the i subscript ranging over banks and firms. No new recruitment nor activity from existing capacity is on the cards. Since we capture balance sheets in the aftermath of a primary issue of equity, we need not assume capital gains. G&L introduce a set of stock-flow norms. For our purposes, we require the dividend yield of firms $r_K = FD_f/(e_{f\text{-}1}p_{f\text{-}1})$ and the price earnings ratio $PE_f = p_f/(F_f/e_{f\text{-}1})$. We have F the realized entrepreneurial profits of production firms. Some part is retained. The rest FD_f is distributed as dividends. In the event that a negligible portion of profits is disbursed as shares so as to finance the investment plans of firms, the first ratio would be almost zero for a given value of the second. The product would be less than one. Since we assume that investment plans are being financed only by fresh infusions of equity, all profits are distributed. We extend G&L's definition to banks symmetrically positioned as financial entities. Thus, introducing the entrepreneurial profits of banks, the dividend yield of banks $r_B = FD_b/e_{b\text{-}1}p_{b\text{-}1}$ and their price earnings ratio $PE_b = p_b/(F_b/e_{b\text{-}1})$. In that case, we have

$$p_f = (r_K PE_f)\, p_{f\text{-}1} \quad \text{and } p_b = (r_B PE_b)\, p_{b\text{-}1}$$

Recall that in the event of almost complete ploughback of profits, both the coefficients above would be strictly less than unity ensuring the stability of the system.

The central bank will calibrate economy-wide speedbreakers. The reserves ratio is imposed on the liabilities of banks but the liabilities of banks in our spartan model are backed by their holdings of commercial paper. The bank liquidity ratio *BLR* is the ratio of assets, shares of companies, to liabilities, own funding of positions. In the terms of our equations, we define $e_f p_f = BLR e_b p_b$.

We propose the following formula connecting them, $\rho = (e_f / e_b . e_{b-1} / e_{f-1})(r_K PE_f) BLR^2$. The justification is not hard to provide. A high liquidity ratio, a fraction (its importance underscored by squaring it), reduces the need for a central bank to impose a high reserves ratio and vice versa.

Our definitions can be represented as

$$\begin{bmatrix} p_f \\ p_b \end{bmatrix} = \begin{bmatrix} r_K PE_f & 0 \\ 0 & \rho \end{bmatrix} \begin{bmatrix} p_{f-1} \\ p_{b-1} \end{bmatrix}$$

The geometry of the phase portrait can be depicted in the trace-determinant plane (T, D). In particular, everything hinges on the sign of $T^2 - 4D$. Since, in either instance, we have a strictly positive value of the trace, we have a spiral source (Hirsch, Smale and Devaney, 2013, p 62). The eigenvalues are complex with nonzero imaginary part if $T^2 - 4D < 0$ and real and distinct if $T^2 - 4D > 0$. Computing and simplifying the expression in our case the sign of the inequality turns out to depend on the sign of $(r_K PE_f)^2 + \rho^2 - 2 r_K PE_f$.

4.2 Firewalls, narrow banking, universal banking

Despite the knife-edge scenario sketched in the previous section, it is possible to prohibit banks from engaging in proprietary trading and arbitrage trading unrelated to the financing of business. The recommendation is to build a firewall between those institutions that create credit through liquidity arbitrage and those that arbitrage credit to engage in risk arbitrage (Kregel, 2010). From a policy perspective, deposit-taking banks must be distinguished from deposit-making banks. Deposit traders must be disallowed from proprietary trading.

Scholars have been poring through the classics afresh hoping to unearth guideposts for a monetary system that is not driven exclusively by the self interest of the butcher, the baker, the candlestick maker (Hillinger, 2010; Krainer, 2010; Rockoff, 2010). According to the real bills doctrine as enunciated by Adam Smith a banker must lend to a borrower only the amount that the borrower would hold as cash. The bank is no more than a ledger. Banks must not lend out for long-term capital investments. Post-Smith this doctrine came to mean the erection of firewalls between investment banking and commercial banking. How would a bank get around the problem of asymmetric information? The advice was to discount bills of exchange. Only a real bill of exchange drawn by a real creditor upon a real debtor which as soon as it comes due is repaid would be acceptable. Smith did not wish real bills to be regulated by the State. A simple prohibition on mortgage loans by commercial banks written into the law, for example, would suffice. Milton Friedman's one-hundred percent reserve banking proposal belonged to the same family in requiring banks to hold one unit of high-powered money for every unit of public deposits. Banks could raise funds by issuing stock and long-term debt. Depositors would be paid a fee not interest. The central bank should pay interest on deposits. Competition between banks would result in a positive interest rate. The public would desire to increase their bank deposits. The central bank would earn seigniorage as the money stock would be determined by it.

One embellishment is for the government to supply checking account money through the central bank. Debits on the central bank with currency would become legal tender. The mechanism would be durable. For private banks might circumvent government regulations and become surreptitious non-bank financial intermediaries (NBFIs) and their shares and claims to assets would not be insured by the government. Checking account services would be priced efficiently. Under the present dispensation, the cost is hidden to depositors in the spread between interest rates charged on the two sides of the balance sheet. However, we are mildly skeptical. Blueprints for free banking have been getting more and more sophisticated and the case for central banks as a counter is not fully developed.

The claim is that shadow banking financed by uninsured claims cannot prosper under this scheme. Since there would be no risk-free government insurance program backing the claims financing these NBFIs, risk-averse investors would demand a higher expected return relative to the prevailing return on insured deposits in banks. The appetite for debt-financed risky real assets by the public would be killed. At the onset of the recent subprime crisis bank reserves everywhere were nearly nil. This was an offshoot of deregulation. Required reserves of commercial banks were steadily reduced. Basel II, for instance, was long on capital structure but short on reserve ratios.

We hold on to the thought that with the prohibitions written into banking law the monetary authority has no degree of freedom reduced by a reserves policy. At the same time, we depart from the Friedman gestalt that the hands of the government must be off investment decisions by banks. We are not sanguine that the private sector along with NPFIs and financial markets would steer the economy towards savings-productive investment balance. We are not indifferent to what happens on the other side of the Chinese wall: the private sector must reap the profits as suffer the loss from risk-taking.

Consider an economy where the government finances its expenditure from income taxes and does not issue long-term paper. We focus on citizens as rentiers so the only source of nominal private income *YP* is the distributed profits of firms *FD* and the interest income from funds parked in banks $r_{m-1}.M_{-1}$. The *M* could well be private money and the attached term is the rate of interest on deposits. Disposable income *YD* is what is left after the taxman has visited and after the loan covenants to the banks $r_{l-1}.L_{h-1}$ have been met. The '*h*' subscript distinguishes bank loans to households. In this bare-bones model (no wage bill, inventory dynamics, and so on), firm profits *F* equal sales *S* which, in turn, must equal $C + G$.

The definition of retained earnings of firms, *FU*, is

$$FU = F - FD - r_{l-1}.L_{f-1} + r_{l-1}.NPL$$

Identical to the discussion of the household, firms have to pay banks back, the subscript '*f*' now marking them. Non-performing loans are *NPL*, as a proportion, *npl*,

$NPL = npl.L_{f-1}$. The term stands for interest payments due to banks that do not reach them. Consequently, profits are increased by that amount.

Putting these identities together relationships like the following are generated.

$$YD = (1-\theta)\ (FU + C + G) + [(1-\theta)r_{m-1}.M_{-1} - \ r_{l-1}.L_{-1}] + r_{l-1}[\theta + (1-\ \theta)NPL]$$

Total loans *L* are the sum of the loans to the two sections of the private sector referred to. Trivially, the first term tells us that disposable income is maximized when the tax rate is zero. The second term, the first in square brackets, is a summary statistic of Glass-Steagall commercial banks squeezed by systemic requirements. In particular, there might be a cap on interest rates charged on loans. There is another inducement in the bracket for the income tax to be negligible. The second term in square brackets cuts two ways. The low tax regime means a high *NPL* term because profits are, to that extent, boosted. The only way to obliterate the term is for the highest tax rate to be applied. Retained earnings of firms would be correspondingly less.

The dynamics of 'originate and hold' banking can be developed with the addition of just one more equation. Fresh investment plans of firms *I* must be supported by retained earnings, new loans, ΔL, and share issue, $\Delta e.p_e$, where p_e. stands for the price of firms' equities. *NPL* will act as a drag on the animal spirits of entrepreneurs. That is to say,

$$\Delta L = I - FU - \Delta e.p_e - NPL$$

We can use the following SFC financial ratios mimicking those for banks in section 4.1, the dividend yield, $r_K = FD/(e_{-1}.p_{e-1})$ and the price earnings ratio $PE = (p_e.e_{-1})/F$.

Combining the definitions, we derive the following dynamic in lending to firms:

Let $r_K(1-\theta) \equiv \gamma$. Then

$$L_f = (1 - npl)L_{f-1} + 1/\gamma[(1-\theta)\, r_{m-1}.M_{-1} - r_{l-1}.L_{h-1}] + [I - FU + F.PE] - YD/\gamma$$

Now NPAs take their natural place as dampening the dynamics of loans to firms. The second term and the first term in square brackets have been encountered in the guise of 'Glass-Steagall commercial banks', only now confined to loans to households. The common denominator gamma was/is a difficulty because it combines a financial variable with a policy variable. In particular, the objective was/is not to allow r_m and r_l to be compared with r_K. A value of $\theta = 1 - 1/r_K$ gives the desired separation. The other supports to loan taking, investment plans, profits and the price earnings ratio, act as expected. The greater the retained earnings, naturally, the lower the recourse to outside funding.

4.3 Virtuous balance sheets in a developing economy

We confine ourselves, to start with, with 'real' magnitudes. Structuralist macroeconomists have expounded the case of two-sector models of developing economies or a breakup of the economy into an industrial and an agricultural sector. For the purposes of the present subsection, the division cuts across the division of the economy into Departments as earlier but, this time, we modify the specification of Kaleçki, 1976. Our Sector I includes Marx's Department II producing luxury goods for capitalists, Sector II is Marx's Department III producing Basics for workers and Department I producing investment goods is divided into two parts, investment goods produced in Sector I and investment goods produced in Sector II. We resort to the modification so as to make Non Basics and Basics output correspond with the output of Sector I and Sector II respectively.

The pricing rule for the industrial sector takes the form

$$P_n = (1 + \tau) w_n b_n$$

where P_n is Sector I's producer price, τ is the markup rate, w_n is the nominal wage rate, and b is the inverse of average labor productivity. Output X_n is divided in the familiar way between consumption and investment. Consistent with the division into Departments above is the assumption that the agriculture sector is a food sector providing Basics to workers in both sectors. Similarly, the industrial sector output is consumed by capitalists from both sectors.

Modern monetary growth models add a Keynes-Wicksell turn in the assumption that firms make their investment plans on the basis of the divergence between the rate of profit in industry r_n and the real rate of return on bonds $i - \pi$ with bonds and equities being regarded as perfect substitutes. Distinguishing the agriculture sector by the subscript a, excess demand in the non-food sector in nominal terms is given by

$$P_n C_n + P_a C_a + P_n I_n (r_n - (i - \pi)) - P_n X_n$$

where C_n is Non Basics consumption by urban capitalists and C_a is luxury consumption by their rural landlord-capitalist-merchant confederates.

Prices are assumed to be flexible in the agricultural sector. We also assume, without loss of generality, that financial portfolio choices are unavailable to the kulaks. Investment in the sector depends only on the rate of profit there. Excess demand in Sector II is

$$w_n L_n + w_a L_a + P_a I_a (r_a) - P_a X_a$$

where $w_i L_i$ is the wage bill in sector i.

We defer dynamical considerations to the next section. For the moment we round off the discussion with companion monetary considerations. The tale that begins with a barter economy and enumerates its infelicities and then goes on to make the case for money may be a bad pedagogical device. On some accounts, money was always, effectively, fiat money (Wray, 2012). A different evolutionary account advanced by advocates of free banking speaks of markets as the natural order of things. In a manner similar to goods and services coming to market in response to the preferences of individuals and the technological blueprints available in society, so too do private purveyors of money emerge. Long epochs of time when private monies circulated and before central banks entered the stage are cited as periods of stability. This case can be challenged on the same lines as the limitations of markets. For instance, negative externalities and public goods call for State action. In one story associated with the economics of Keynes, macroeconomics is a coordination problem. Even in an economy with atomistic agents and with a propensity to cooperate there are social outcomes that will be unattainable. The monetary authorities can step in with fiat money as a coordinating device. The paper is intrinsically worthless. Money until recently, Michael Woodford defining practice, had been evicted from the mainstream model (McCallum, 2012). The rationale was that some medium of exchange and store of value would evolve as agents went about their business maximizing their utilities. There was no reason to pay special attention to monetary aggregates. At the same time, since the monetary authorities intervene in markets at the behest of the fiscal authorities, they influence a price, the rate of interest, that is an ingredient in the inter temporal choices of agents. Pushing the point home to its logical conclusion, if the fiscal authorities balance their budgets, reason for central banks on that account evaporates. Private banks will spawn to smoothen the lifetime plans of freely-contracting individuals. Their programs would be the duals of those of households and firms. In the end, transversality conditions of all parties must intermesh. Liabilities and assets will eventually match. Private money will be backed at the terminal date. Of course, this line of thinking unraveled in 2008 with backward induction on plans made for very short horizons. The monetary policy maker reappeared larger than life and Michael Woodford led the retreat back into the theory of central bank balance sheets.

The challenge, then, is to contend with the limitations of markets with fiat money that is unbacked. Robert Shiller has a backed-money proposal that has commodity baskets behind the consumer price index. We propose the following scheme of fully-backed central bank money building on the acclaimed rural employment guarantee scheme in India. Imagine that it is extended to all seeking dignified employment at a decent wage (say by ILO standards). In the language of macroeconomics, let the average wage be w and the number of the unemployed be N. Then the total wage bill to embark on an employment-generation effort is wN. The central bank acts as "employer of last resort" providing the base money to support this social enterprise. The financial intermediaries though which this regime would be effected are regional rural banks or cooperative banks. Their assets would be public-private projects that meet scrupulous cost-benefit standards and the liabilities would be the wages of the workers. For instance, in the UK the Green Investment Bank or a nationalized bank (an institution which more and more policy makers as in Brazil and elsewhere are looking back at wistfully) could issue bonds purchasable by the Bank of England (Ryan-Collins et al, 2016). In Germany the connections are symbiotic. 70% of the deposits come from over 1000 local small-savings and cooperative banks. Their clientele is the household and SME sector. The collapse of the local banking system in the country would be halted and reversed. Formally, $wN = M$. Since the propensity to consume wage goods by the working class is, by definition unity, their incomes return to firms who redeem their debts to the financial intermediaries. In an accounting sense, there is no need for a rate of interest. Money refluxes back to its issuer.

We round off this discussion with a glimpse of the fascinating work of historians who are overturning received wisdom using sophisticated concepts and refined sources of data. Thus, the industrial revolution in popular perceptions is captured by notions of scientific advance and creative genius. It turns out, though, that modern economic growth began two centuries earlier than hitherto recorded and was the outcome of an "Industrious Revolution" (Humphries & Weisdorf, 2016). Succinctly put, Britain's industrial revolution was 1% inspiration and 99% perspiration. It was the continuous increase in the length of the working year and the intensification of this process prior to industrialization that was the prime mover. The basic explanation might be choice in one direction along the work-leisure tradeoff or more structural causes like the vanishing of alternatives to wage labour and shifts in the balance of bargaining power.

4.4 Short circuits and crises

The so-called Keynesian or Marshallian adjustment process flips the Walrasian tâtonnement adjustment process. Quantities are assumed to adjust to quantity discrepancies assuming chronic excess capacity. In the case of the formulation of the previous section, we have

$$\frac{dX_n}{dt} = \left[P_n C_n + P_a C_a + P_n (I_n (r_n - (i - \pi)) - P_n X_n\right]$$

The agricultural sector, on the other hand, is resource-constrained. An increase in the supply of food can only come from investment activities like irrigation works and so on. The adjustment rule for the agricultural sector is

$$\frac{dP_a}{dt} = \left[w_n L_n + w_a L_a + P_a I_a (r_a) - P_a X_a\right]$$

The Jacobian of the system is

$$\begin{pmatrix} -P_n & C_a \\ 0 & I_a - X_a \end{pmatrix}$$

Recalling the stability criteria spelt out in Section 4.1, our solution is a sink if the trace of the matrix is strictly negative. This means, $I_a < X_a + P_n$. Taking each item in turn, skyrocketing prices of luxuries might shrink demand for the output of that sector releasing labour for employment in the Basics sector. A high level of the marketable surplus in agriculture is the sine qua non of the inequality (for a 'low' value of I_a). Of it, a sizable chunk must be devoted to the consumption of Basics (tucked away in the north-east corner of the box). Our theme of a State-driven wage-led growth strategy recurs. The challenge of maintaining full employment under falling aggregate growth has been met with simulations with SFC models (Jackson et al, 2016). The key is labour-intensive technology. It is not possible to take policy stances on the productivity of labour. The government could initiate the structural change in the desired direction. Service sectors like the care of the young and elderly, for example, generate value by the time people spend in them. The State would need to protect the quality and intensity of the time devoted in these workspaces. The worldwide proportion of jobs that are performed unregistered by the State is high and increasing. In developing countries, the share may be higher than half of all non-agricultural jobs and up to 90% if the agricultural sector is included. One view is that productivity is impaired (Dreschler et al, 2008). The competitiveness of an economy is reduced as informal firms stay small for reasons to do with tax and labour laws. Their access to inputs like credit is limited and they cannot forge formal business relationships. Another position is that informal means innovative with flexibility. There are, in addition, public finance concerns. Revenues are obviously reduced. The ability to develop social security systems based on taxation and contributions is affected. Mariana Mazzucato has pioneered the theory and practice of State-inspired technical progress according to a Plan (Mazzucato & Semieniuk, 2017). The *loci classici* are the works of Keynes, Schumpeter, and Minsky. History displays an inversion of means and ends, the origin and nature of finance will determine investments made. The perspective is macro and "mission-oriented" towards climate change, depletion of resources, healthcare. Results are supply-push (R&D) and demand-pull (employment and diffusion). Cleverly positioned entry snowballs into effects all along the innovation change, from basic science to applications to seed-funding of companies culminating in procurement policies. The contrast with micro reasoning is sharp. Towards the end of a standard course, "market failures" are introduced. Innovations would figure as a prominent illustration of "positive externalities" However, the historical record here, connecting explicitly with the systems precepts in our Introduction, provides evidence of the "market-making and market-shaping" role played by public authorities. Policies have spelt out technological blueprints and sectors, innovations in agriculture not excluded, in which the dynamics of the Plan would play out. To employ another metaphor, the playing field would have to be tilted in favour of the Department of prime interest and against Departments of less interest. Most high-growth innovative companies receive their head start in high-risk finance from venture funds in public banks, for instance, rather than private venture capitalists.

Rural non-farm employment accounts for 35% to 45% percent of income among rural households worldwide. It is regarded as a means of creating fresh employment opportunities, increasing and smoothening income flows, and arresting the rural-to-urban migration in areas where the movement is not recommended (Jonasson, 2008). With most of the world experiencing no more than mild inflation, an assault on an imaginary enemy with the modern weapon of the bank rate would be unnecessary. Indeed, high inflation hurts financial interests (Irwin, 2008; McKinley, 2008). Bankers lose because their mortgages and other fixed-interest securities they hold as assets dwindle in value. Mild inflation favours the majority. Households who hold mortgages and small businesses indebted to banks benefit. As long as the government and the trade unions subscribe to a wage policy that does not entail wage erosion, a slowly increasing price level will not harm working class interests.

Chapter 5

Europe

Europe is every macroeconomist's favourite testing ground. Even in a non-experimental discipline, the entry and exit of members and the plethora of reasons provide regular fodder for the making and unmaking of hypotheses. The contours of this history in the making are well known: monetary union without fiscal and banking union, "strong" (Germany) and "weak" (Greece) countries rubbing shoulders in contrast to the textbook requirements for a monetary union. We build up towards a synthetic and novel policy recommendation in the third section, working slowly through the first two.

5.1 Monetary Union and Fiscal Pacts

Public debt is vitally different from private debt (Wray, 2011). An individual cannot pay off her debt by using her own IOUs. Usually a third party like a bank intermediates in the payment of individual debt. When a sovereign country, on the other hand, is presented with its own IOU it promises to exchange it for another IOU. Alternatively, it allows the presenter to "redeem" it in payment of taxes. A State can never default as long as it does not pledge to redeem its IOUs on demand to the IOUs of a foreign country. A private debt is destroyed when a loan is repaid. Fiat money is destroyed when taxes are paid. While the creation of private debt and commodity production depends on optimism, the issue of fiat money does not. The government must step in when private enterprise falters keeping output and employment operating at capacity. To that end, flexible exchange rates are indispensable. A Eurozone country cannot manage its public debt when it is denominated in a currency that the country does not control. It is akin to holding foreign-denominated debt (Pérez-Caldentey & Vernengo, 2012). A government must be in control of its own currency and cannot do so when it is obliged to redeem its currency at a fixed price.

We can put the issue sharply using the G&C schemata. Money is introduced on two separate occasions. Even in the event of a drying up of investment projects in the pipeline, firms and banks must come together to finance the dynamics of inventory accumulation or decumulation. Thus, a fresh flow of bank money for the purpose is given by $\Delta FA = \Delta I$. Indeed, the first SFC norm in the G&C set and the most important is alpha and, outside the steady state,

$FA = \alpha FE$ (G&C, 1983, p 93), where FE is private expenditure. In words, in every period the ratio of the end-period bank money stock to private expenditure equals the "money-income norm". Also, the excess of government expenditure over government income is financed by money creation. That is to say, $G - YG = \Delta GD$. G&C then relabel FA as PD, private debt or bank lending to the private sector, and define $\Delta FA = \Delta GD + \Delta PD$.

It is clear that a Greek fiscal deficit, for instance, cannot coexist with an independent European Central Bank. The matter is best visualized in the second fundamental G&C cum Post Keynesian equation, the equality of the government deficit and the private sector surplus. Using superscripts for dramatic effect, we have (G&C, 1983, pp 105-106)

$$YP^{Greece} - (PE^{Greece} + \Delta \underline{I}^{Greece}) = G^{Greece} - YG^{Greece} = \Delta FA^{Europe} - \Delta PD^{Greece}$$

We could pack the extreme left-hand side with SFC norms underlining G&C's sensitivity to the details of the domestic production process. There could be, for instance, γ which is the ratio of opening inventories to final sales in each period I_{-1}/PE, g which is the proportional change in inventories in each period $\Delta I = gI_{-1}$ (G&C, p 95). Coming to the equation in the centre, the fiscal stance of the Greek government comes to naught if the increase in Euros on the extreme right-hand side is null.

5.2 Euro-area bonds

In the present context, some have recommended that only nationals buy government bonds (Koo, 2011). The case is made thus. Up until a few years ago, after the telecom bubble burst in 2000, banks in Germany bought the debt of southern European countries because they offered higher yields than domestic debt. Note that the currency of denomination was the same, the euro. The capital inflow from Germany fuelled the housing bubble in those countries. The flow has now gone into reverse. Fixed-income fund managers in Spain and Ireland are buying German government bonds because they find their own country's fiscal positions untenable. To emphasise, they do not face exchange rate risk. The result is that the governments of these countries cannot access the savings surpluses of their citizens

A case for monetary-fiscal coordination can, in fact, be made with general equilibrium tools. One of the key institutional elements in such a recent blueprint for Europe is a non-defaultable Eurobond labeled a "euro area fund" (Corsetti et al, 2016). "Non-defaultable" means that the fund and the ECB would stand by ready to convert maturing Eurobonds into currency at par. The fund would buy the national debt of each member country subject to each state meeting specified fiscal criteria. Suppose a fiscal authority undertakes a set of measures to reduce the present value of the primary surplus. In the event, the real value of the debt must correspondingly fall. The price level will increase by implication and assuming price-setting behavior output will expand in the short run. The multiplier effects can be considerable. In order to be successful, it is imperative that monetary policy accommodate the fiscal action by keeping interest rates low. In the event of an unsuccessful auction sale of government bonds to banks and the non-bank public, the central bank must step in. If fiscal policy makes the primary surplus rise with the real value of government bonds even if entirely held by the central bank, an expansion in the monetary base to buy these bonds will leave the wealth of private agents unaffected relative to the primary surplus. Consider, on the other hand, the other extreme when fiscal policy makes the primary surplus respond to the real value of government bonds held by the private sector. In this case, a permanent increase in the monetary base to finance these purchases by the central bank increases the wealth of private agents relative to the primary surplus. The reason is that the primary surplus falls as the quantity of government bonds in the hands of the public declines. The positive wealth activity is likely to boost activity.

Consider the dynamics of the long-term bond. The government issues long-term bonds *BL*. Assume that only households accept the offerings. To the other two items in disposable income in the current period BL_{-1} must be added. Consumers now earn capital gains $CG = \Delta p_{bL}.BL + \Delta p_e.e_{-1}$ on their financial assets where $p_{bL}(= 1/r_{bL},$ the yield on long-period bonds) is the price of perpetuities. Haig-Simons disposable income $YD_{hs} = YD + CG$. The government deficit or public sector borrowing requirement $PSBR = \Delta BL.p_{bL}$. We introduce fiat money and the connection between high-powered money supplied to the banks H_b and deposits introduced above is the cash reserve ratio ρ. Finally, government debt $GD = BL + H$. This is enough to derive the following difference equation in government bonds:

$$BL = (1 + (r_{bL}.r_{m-1})/\rho)BL_{-1} - r_{bL}\underline{FD}(1 - 1/r_K) + r_{bL.}YD_{hs} + r_{bL}(PSBR - r_{m-1}/\rho GD_{-1}) \\ - r_{bL}.PE.F$$

Clubbing all the 'public sector' terms with the same sign on one side and the 'private sector' terms with the opposite sign on the other, we recognize a variant of the familiar macroeconomic identity: a private sector surplus equals a public sector deficit.

5.3 Tax-backed bonds, Geuros: the money-bond continuum

We generalise the Mosler and Pilkington (2013) scheme across time and space. G&L is used for the purpose. Bonds therein are one end of a scale with money at the other. A 'Greek Central Bank' (GCB) mediates in the circulation of these instruments. Stock-flow norms emerge naturally on both sides of its balance sheet. Their ranges determine the stability of the domestic economy.

We appraise and go beyond the innovative tax-backed bonds scheme proposed by Mosler and Pilkington (Pilkington, 2013, is an elaboration). The origin was the outright monetary transactions (OMT) program announced by the ECB on August 2, 2012, that ensured unlimited financing in the form of freshly-minted money to suppress sovereign debt yields. However, the policy was tied to an austerity package. Our Post Keynesian construction respects all the elements in the package, not excluding 'backing', and is not confined to the European experience. In contrast, Mosler and Pilkington emphasise that in situations when governments do not renege on their payments commitments, the tax element vanishes. An additional fillip is provided by Paul de Grauwe who has recently calculated that Greece is solvent but not illiquid (de Grauwe, 2016). Consequently, the current policy of the ECB that OMT support would only be provided to countries that are solvent but illiquid condemns Greece to the pit of a bad equilibrium. We round off the discussion recently initiated by Papadimitriou et al (2015) (2016) for a regime shift in Greece. They use a stock-flow-consistent model to offer two monetary-fiscal proposals. Our discussion as well is confined to G&L on the subject. The second, the Tax Certificates Proposal, is akin to Tax-Backed Bonds. The first is the introduction of a zero-coupon bond, the Geuro. The quantity of Geuro liquidity would have to be precisely calibrated and the task, consequently, is best left to the GCB. Thus, the Geuros would be accepted by the government for tax payments. Our discussion connects both proposals.

5.3.1 Geuros and Greek Central Bank Bills

G&L move freely between bills and bonds. Money financing of the deficit comes first. Our next equation introduced in Section 3.1 is broad brushstroke to fiscal currency (Amato et. al., 2016). The letter H standing for high-powered money or the money base, Geuros held by households and commercial banks as reserves, we have

$$\Delta H = G - T \qquad 34$$

Bills, like bonds, are debt instruments issued by governments in any given period so as to support the budget deficit. They are short-term paper of typically the duration of a year in contrast to government bonds which, in principle, have an infinite life. Here, we assume that bills are held only by commercial banks and the GCB distinguished by recognisable subscripts. Indeed, government paper would be the preferred habitat of conservative investors (Subrun & Turner, 2015). Thus, the existing stock of bills at time *t*, $B_t = B_{bt} + B_{cbt}$. The government budget constraint must include the interest rate payments due on bills held by the two aforementioned parties in the last period. Denoting the rate of interest on bills by r_b, we have

$$\Delta B = G - T + r_{bt-1} B_{bt-1} - r_{bt-1} B_{cbt-1} \qquad 35$$

Comparing equations 34 and 35, the former consists entirely of flow terms, fresh emissions of cash as the right-hand side demands, the periods unconnected with each other. In the case of bill financing, on the other hand, debts incurred on the stock of outstanding bills, usually a staggering figure, must be honoured. Since past and present are connected, the stability of the dynamic arrangement must be established.

Returning to our public sector borrowing requirement (PSBR) in the form of bill financing, we can break up the new sale of bills into its constituent holders. Thereby, we arrive at the following difference equations: $B_{bt} = (1 + r_{bt-1})B_{bt-1}$ and $B_{cbt} = (1 - r_{bt-1})B_{cbt-1}$. The two are distinguished by a positive/negative sign. The GCB is one arm of the Greek government, the other being the Treasury. Furthermore, the GCB is not in the business of making profits. Earnings on holdings of Treasury bills, therefore, are returned to the Treasury. The requirement of stability is that the bracketed terms be less than unity. The condition is naturally met in the case of the GCB, prompting the interpretation of the residual holding of government paper as a built-in stabilizer. A ruthless market rewrite of this convention and one that is insensitive to the rhythms of the cycle would have the GCB free, along with the private sector, to reject the offering of government securities. Indeed, the autonomy of central banks from the government is sought precisely to check the PSBR of the latter.

Since the rate of interest must turn negative for stability of the equation of bank holdings of government paper, we must recall the cyclical context of the discussion. Discriminating government expenditure causes, other things being equal, an increase in private expenditure. Growing private incomes, in turn, lead to larger tax collections and as the upswing gains momentum, our equations go into reverse. Deficits turn to surpluses. We can employ the realm of incentives and evasion with a "fiscal social contract" which Greek citizens can implicitly enter into according to which welfare-enhancing expenditures are provided in exchange for tax payments (Lenton et al, 2017). The model is the opposite of the coercive relationship assumed to exist between taxpayer and State. Otherwise put, under "linked taxation" schemes modelled as leader-follower games, the Greek government would play first either through its expenditures or explicitly display that the burden of taxation is being borne by the wealthy or that the regime is (re)orienting itself towards a progressive taxation structure.

On the other hand, if period-by-period stability is the criterion, elements will have to be found in the balance sheets of banks. It turns out that more than one buffer exist there. We underline the importance of the "acceptance function" of banks that transform the illiquid liabilities of households and firms into their own liabilities (Nersiyan, 2015). Thereby, banks simultaneously create liquidity and support the capital development of a country. To those ends, it is imperative that risks be held on the balance sheets of banks. Denoting the aggregate of deposits by M, the bank liquidity ratio BLR is defined as B_b/M. A time-varying BLR can provide the required stability. Substituting deposits for the difference equation in B_{bt}, we get $M_t = (1 + r_{bt-1})(BLR_{t-1}/BLR_t)M_{t-1}$. We do not have to await the upturn for the stability requirements to be met. No variable need enter negative territory here. The BLR would have to be calibrated with the bill rate across time. For example, suppose that at time period t -1, $r_{bt-1} = 2$, and $BLR_{t-1} = 1/8$. In that case, the bank liquidity ratio in the current period BLR_t must not be less than ½. We respond here to the regulatory requirement that central bank policies should be 'data-dependent', acting and reacting to the state of the world period by period (Subrun & Turner, 2015). In addition, let L stand for the gross loan portfolio of banks. In that case, the capital adequacy ratio is $CAR = M/L$. Taking the product of the two ratios introduced, $BLR.CAR = B_b/L$. In a procedure similar to the one just followed, we can write down our equation of bank holdings of bills in terms of bank loans thus,

$L_t = (1 + r_{bt-1})(CAR_{t-1}BLR_{t-1}/CAR_tBLR_t)L_{t-1}$. Now, two stock-flow norms can be combined with the short-run rate of interest so as to deliver stability.

5.3.2 Government Bonds and Inflation

Policy interest rates too are points on the real number line. At one end is, literally, an overnight rate, a price at which commercial banks can secure funds so as to adhere to reserve requirements. The GCB will support banks that are solvent but facing temporary liquidity problems at a non-penal interest rate. Open-market operations involve the buying and selling of short-term government paper. Until the financial crisis in the US, the rate of interest on bills was regarded as the policy rate par excellence. In standard accounts, the short rate is connected to the long rate by a yield curve. The monetary authorities might wish to bend the curve but always by operating on the short end of the connection.

We proceed to include both the short rate and the long rate in a consistent accounting framework. First, we focus on the short rate. In the familiar model, the target is the inflation rate. The need for including inflation might be questioned given the relevance of the discussion to Europe and, indeed, any part of the world. The inflation beast has been tamed. If anything, deflationary spirals can be spotted here and there. However, in the interest of generality we use G&L's consistent accounting framework to connect the short and the long rate through an array of macroeconomic variables not excluding the inflation rate. In order to focus on the rate of interest on bills, we ignore government bonds for the moment and recall equation 35. We need to flesh out the tax term there in the following elaboration.

$$\Delta B = G - \theta WB + r_{bt-1} B_{bt-1} - r_{bt-1} B_{cbt-1} \qquad 36$$

G&L offer an extensive menu of cost formulae for studying inflation over Chapter 8. For the task on hand, we use the definition of unit costs of production $UC = WB/pr$ where pr stands for the productivity of labor. In that case, the rate of cost inflation is

$\pi_c = UC/UC_{-1}$ -1. Assuming no change in labor productivity in the period under consideration, applying these definitions to equation 36 we get

$$\Delta B = G - \theta(\pi_c + 1) WB_{-1} + r_{bt-1} B_{bt-1} - r_{bt-1} B_{cbt-1} \qquad 37$$

In the steady state, this equation is

$$G = \theta(\pi_c + 1) WB_{-1} + r_{bt-1} B_{bt-1} - r_{bt-1} B_{cbt-1} \qquad 38$$

A critical role in the long-run growth dynamics of the G&L framework is played by the "fiscal stance" (G&L, p 72). It is defined by the steady-state ratio of government expenditure to its income share. We are tempted to express equation 38 as something similar. Accordingly, we define the (inflation-adjusted) *monetary-fiscal stance* as follows

$$WB_{-1} = (G + r_{bt-1}B_{cbt-1} - r_{bt-1}B_{bt-1}) / \theta(\pi_c + 1) \qquad 39$$

We turn now to the long rate. The ECB is at the heart of a project to anchor long-run private sector expectations (Bibow, 2015; Braun, 2015). The ECB's control of long-term interest rates depends on its ability to finetune short-term rates as well satisfy the expectations of the private sector as it writes its imagined future. For the purpose, announcements are less evocative than the actual transmission of policy changes through banks and households and firms. We recall our observations in Section 3.2 on Keynes' case for direct central bank control of the long-term rate in the *Treatise on Money*. Therein, in the case of what we would now call perfect credibility, the GCB can gently steer banks in the direction led by the long rate without actually purchasing bonds itself. In Geoffrey Ingham's development of the Weberian concept of the central bank, the GCB must approach the highest form of rationality that undergirds private sector expectations. This it can do by working with norms banks and households and firms can embrace when each forms expectations of the expectations of the others. Outcomes will always be subjected to incalculable uncertainties but through its decisions and actions the GCB can craft rules of the game that generate mutually-consistent expectations. In the aftermath of the financial crisis in the US, among other extraordinary measures taken the Federal Reserve began to operate at the other end of the spectrum, in the market for government bonds. Elsewhere, the measure has been described as "forward guidance" of the economy. The Greek government issue of bonds at the current market price is $\Delta BL.p_{bL}$. In order to focus, we work with Chapter 3 in G&L, Geuros but not private bank money. From the chapter, we also borrow $Y = WB$. We assume that Greek government bills are held exclusively by local households. That is, $B_t = B_{ht}$. Adding bonds to our equations for bills, 35 or 36, with the modifications, we get

$$\Delta B = B - B_{-1} = (G + r_{bt-1}.B_{ht-1} + BL_{-1}) - \theta Y + \Delta BL.p_{bL} \qquad 40$$

Government bonds add to the wealth V of households in two senses. The return on and the capital gains earned on the holding of bonds have been introduced. The other item of wealth is the interest accruing on their holdings of government bills, $r_{h-1}.B_{h-1}$. Subtracting taxes and consumption from national income, the net accumulation of household wealth is given by

$$\Delta V = (Y - \theta Y - C) + r_{h-1}.B_{h-1} + BL_{-1} + \Delta p_{bL}.BL_{-1} \qquad 41$$

Now,

$$\Delta BL\Delta p_{bL} = \Delta BLp_{bL} + BL\Delta p_{bL} \qquad 42$$

Using 42 when subtracting 41 from 40,

$$\Delta B + \Delta p_{bL}.\Delta BL = C + G + \Delta V - Y \qquad 43$$

In the steady state, we get $Y = C + G$. One again, we crosscheck that our basic identity is restored as well as affirm that the Greek government with all its macroeconomic weapons in readiness is the bedrock of support of the Greek economy. Fiscal policy is essential to the monetary reproduction of the capitalist economy (Davanzati, 2015). Public expenditure injects liquidity and fiscal policy, of which it is a part, anchors capitalist expectations. Policy rates of interest, both short and long, must be considered along with other elements of government policy, expenditure and taxes, to deliver a dynamically stable economy (Ford Foundation/Levy Economics Institute, 2012). More than one calculation shows that fiscal multipliers are higher than previously assumed (Bayoumi, 2015). If monetary policy assumes wider sets of instruments and targets, not excluding domestic asset prices and lending, the case for aligning with fiscal policy as a countercyclical stance becomes stronger.

We have looked to the future of Greece and Europe for inspiration in working with the G&L money-bonds continuum. However, the reference in section 3.2 is not the only occasion when Farley Grubb has energetically expounded the thesis that the connection can be sought in the past (Grubb, 2016). Virginia's paper money functioned as a zero-coupon bond. It was created by the legislature and spent by it through the Treasury. With ease of use, it assumed medium-of-exchange functions. That is to say, citizens reduced the discount rate they attached to the notes, initiating the transition of the notes to the traits of fiat money. Grubb employs a multi-period version of our equation 34 to record budget deficits and surpluses over the cycle. A transversality condition is imposed to ensure budget balance in the end. Colonial paper money Acts included concurrent tax legislation designed to redeem the notes emitted at their face value. Redeemed notes were removed from circulation and destroyed.

We started out with the Pilkington & Mosler-Papadimitriou et al out-of-the-box bonds schemes designed to lift Europe/Greece out of the crisis into which they have sunk. Our intent was to embed the policy in fully-specified models that the authors were also using. The Godley-Lavoie framework is robust to all phases of the cycle. Bonds are one end of a continuum, money-bills-bonds. Our logic led through the commercial banking system to the economy as a whole. Deposits are the savings of households and loans are disbursed to both households and firms. Connecting them are norms concerning liquidity and capital adequacy which are at the forefront of academic and practical discussion. Our formulations were designed to draw out stability conditions for different representations.

Chapter 6

Companion micro foundations

The present chapter is the companion to Chapter 3, fulfilling the promises made there. To wit, we solve out the optimization exercises deriving the demand and supply functions introduced. The end is constructive. Taking first-order conditions gives us fairly precise policy orientations.

6.1 The dynamics of agrarian transformation

We make the case for a large-scale employment scheme providing dignified employment at a decent wage in a dynamic sector. The sector is agriculture following the case made in sections 3.1 and 4.4. In one line of thinking, the industrial sector not just prospectively but retrospectively might not be (have been) suited to the task (Dadush, 2016; Franck & Galor, 2015). The factors that fostered industrialization elsewhere were elements exclusive to the West. In the long run the thesis goes, industrialization has a less-than-salutary effect on the skill intensity of the production process. Constructively then, industrial policy must identify opportunities to boost investment, productivity, employment, across all sectors. Manufacturing typically accounts for 10% to 15% of employment in developing countries and far less in the US and many advanced economies. It is falling in relative importance as a source of value addition and employment. The demand for manufactures is subject to low and falling income elasticity of demand and manufacturing is susceptible to automation. In sum, the long-term value added and employment trends are beginning to resemble agriculture. In other fresh looks at industrialization, successful industrialisers have been identified as those that met two criteria connected with the skills of the labour force (Kelly et al, 2015). They had a large number of small farms and were connected with superior nutrition and height. Secondly, a high density of the rural population in these cases suggested deep rural industry. These countries already depended on the extensive technical and entrepreneurial skills generated thereby. In short, early industrialization was less about adopting new technologies than adapting labour-using techniques to the stage where they generate profits.

Different class configurations in different regions had a role to play as regions recovered from the shocks of the late medieval period (Karayalcin, 2015). The second phase of the Agricultural Revolution was marked by the appropriation of the food surplus by an expropriating class (Tisdell & Svizzero, 2015). The attendant development of States eventually culminated in centralized economic systems. The lesson to be learnt is that the dynamics of development is less about per capita income and more about the accumulation of capital and innovation. In Western Europe, peasant proprietors tilled small plots. The increase in population led to lower real wages. Since the incomes of landlords were not relatively high either, the result was low demand for manufactured goods. In Eastern Europe, in contrast, second serfdom kept wages low but rents high. Since however the class of landlords was small, demand for manufactures was weak. Northwestern Europe fell between these polar cases. Rising wages and rents triggered an increase in manufacturing activity. In fresh looks at history, the peasantry has been rehabilitated as an engine of growth (Kopsidis & Ivanov, 2015). Agricultural revolutions did not precede industrial revolutions in Western & Central Europe in the 19th century but occurred simultaneously. Both agricultural and industrial productivities rose sharply in seventeenth century England (Wallis et al, 2016). Industry fuelled agriculture, not the other way around. Today, as then, accelerated agricultural development is demand-driven, depending on the long-term demand for food from an expanding non-agricultural sector. The agrarian transformation of the title depends upon improved productivity and the ability of industry to absorb the agricultural surplus. The first condition is predicated on the diffusion of land-saving, labor-using technologies through the alignment of peasants and public policy. The second requires employment growth in the secondary sector. At another end, digital technologies mean few jobs, inadequate investment and spending (Frey, 2015). The jobs to be encouraged are solar photovoltaic installers, wind engineers, biofuels product managers.

Fresh reads of finance are relevant. Tawney's critique of Weber's thesis to the proposition that banking and long-distance credit laid the foundation of the Reformation is gathering respect (Becker et al, 2016). McCloskey later was to flesh out the proposition to offer innovation, not accumulation, as the prime mover of capitalist penetration in the West. In short, scholars propose that revolutions are possible when a confluence of supply-side elements allow challenges to the *ancien regime* to pass through successfully. The demand for the Reformation was dormant for centuries prior to the arrival of Luther. However, the success of the Reformers of the 16th century depended on timing and situation. Information technology in the form of the printing press facilitated coordination through forging networks of sympathizers. At the same time, the penetration of sophisticated finance into agriculture is a matter of pressing and contemporary concern (Russi & Ferrando, 2015). Forwards and futures markets there (and anywhere) are prone to self-referential dynamics that have no connection with the fundamentals of demand and supply. The alternative perspective in contrast to looking at pieces of land as assets to be traded in international markets is based on "food sovereignty" taken to mean the complex engagement of the peasant with the environment, the reproduction of the conditions of production grounded in local innovations, and knowhow.

We express our problem in the language of differential games of Dockner, Jørgensen, Van Long and Sorger (2000). Equation 27 is transformed into the dynamical system

$$\dot{N}(t) = (1+n)\left(\frac{k(t)}{1-w(t)}\right)\left\{g_{p_{ut}} + \left(1+\frac{1}{p_{ut}}\right)v_{ut}\right\}N(t), N(0) = N_0$$

The conflict here is that between capitalists-entrepreneurs, choosing $k(t)$ to maximize their payoffs in conflict with workers-households who chose $w(t)$ to maximize their (indirect) utility. This stark description can be enriched by a political economy typology according to which this particular modus has been labeled "contract farming" (Banaji, 2016). The conflict here is between industrial capital and the efforts of households in the countryside to resist proletarianisation. Accordingly, the profit function of the former is

$$J^C = \int_0^T e^{-r_c t}\pi^C\big(N(t), k(t), w(t)\big)dt \qquad 44$$

and the utility function of the latter is

$$J^W = \int_0^T e^{-r_w t}v^W\big(N(t), k(t), w(t)\big)dt \qquad 45$$

We proceed to derive the open-loop Nash Equilibrium of the game

The capitalist Hamiltonian is

$$H^C = \pi^C\big(N(t), k(t), w(t)\big) + \lambda(t)\left[(1+n)\left(\frac{k(t)}{1-w(t)}\right)\left\{g_{p_{ut}} + \left(1+\frac{1}{p_{ut}}\right)v_{ut}\right\}N(t)\right] \qquad 46$$

Maximizing with respect to the capital stock per worker, the quantity and price of the other inputs given at optimal levels,

$$p_{ut} = -\lambda(t)\left[(1+n)\left(\frac{1}{1-w(t)}\right)\left\{g_{p_{ut}} + \left(1+\frac{1}{p_{ut}}\right)v_{ut}\right\}N(t)\right] \qquad 47$$

Recourse is taken to the envelope property of the payoff function. The values of the quantity and price of the other inputs given at optimal levels, the derivative of the Lagrangian with respect to capital equals price. Plugging this expression into the Hamiltonian, the maximized Hamiltonian is

$$H^{C*} = \pi^C\big(N(t), k(t), w(t)\big) - p_{ut} \qquad 48$$

The adjoint equation is

$$\begin{aligned}\dot{\lambda}(t) &= r_c\lambda(t) - H_N^{C*} \\ &= r_c\lambda(t) - w(t)\end{aligned} \qquad 49$$

The derivative of the profit function with respect to the level of employment, other things being optimal, is the wage rate. The solution of the equation is

$$\lambda(t) = -e^{\int r_c(t)dt}\int e^{\int r_c(t)dt}w(t)dt \qquad 50$$

Coming to the worker, her Hamiltonian is

$$H^W = v^W\big(N(t), k(t), w(t)\big) + \mu(t)\left[(1+n)\left(\frac{k(t)}{1-w(t)}\right)\left\{g_{p_{ut}} + \left(1+\frac{1}{p_{ut}}\right)v_{ut}\right\}N(t)\right] \qquad 51$$

Maximizing with respect to the wage,

$$N(t) = \mu(t)\left[(1+n)\left(\frac{k(t)}{[1-w(t)]^2}\right)\left\{g_{p_{ut}} + \left(1+\frac{1}{p_{ut}}\right)v_{ut}\right\}N(t)\right] \qquad 52$$

The connection between the indirect utility function and the profit function is Hôtelling's lemma. The supply function of labour equals the demand function of labour, $N(t) = -\frac{\partial \pi^C}{\partial w(t)}$. Substituting this expression into the Hamiltonian, we get the maximized Hamiltonian for the worker.

$$H^{W*} = v^W\big(N(t), k(t), w(t)\big) - N(t) \qquad 53$$

The adjoint equation in this case is

$$\dot{\mu}(t) = r_w\mu(t) - H_N^{W*}$$
$$= r_w\mu(t) - w(t) + 1 \qquad 54$$

Disutility is increasing in employment. In equilibrium, the marginal utility of labour equals the wage. The solution of this equation is

$$\mu(t) = e^{\int r_w(t)dt} \int e^{\int r_w(t)dt}(1 - w(t))dt \qquad 55$$

We will comment on shadow prices later so we note that the term in brackets on the right-hand side is positive by definition.

We turn now to the computation of the Markovian Nash Equilibrium of the game.

In order to facilitate comparison between the two solution sets the same numbers for the equations are used, a practice that will continue for the following exercises as well. Single and double and triple primes will distinguish closed-loop and open-loop expressions. The capitalist this time works on the assumption that the worker's strategy depends on the state of the world, $w\big(N(t)\big)$. The Hamiltonian in this case is

$$H^C = \pi^c\big(N(t), k(t), w(N(t))\big) + \lambda(t)\left[(1+n)\left(\tfrac{k(t)}{1-w(N(t))}\right)\left\{g_{p_{ut}} + \left(1 + \tfrac{1}{p_{ut}}\right)v_{ut}\right\}N(t)\right] \qquad 46'$$

Once again, maximizing with respect to the capital stock per worker,

$$p_{ut} = -\lambda(t)\left[(1+n)\left(\tfrac{1}{1-w(N(t))}\right)\left\{g_{p_{ut}} + \left(1 + \tfrac{1}{p_{ut}}\right)v_{ut}\right\}N(t)\right] \qquad 47'$$

Substituting this expression into the Hamiltonian, the maximized Hamiltonian is

$$H^{C*} = \pi^{C}\big(N(t), k(t), w(N(t))\big) - p_{ut} \qquad 48'$$

The adjoint equation is

$$\begin{aligned}\dot{\lambda}(t) &= r_c\lambda(t) - H_N^{C*}\\ &= r_c\lambda(t) - w(N(t)) - \pi_w^C(N(t), k(t), w(N(t))w_N'(N(t)) \qquad 49'\end{aligned}$$

The solution of the equation is

$$\lambda(t) = -e^{\int r_c(t)dt} \int e^{\int r_c(t)dt}(w(N(t)) + \pi_w^C w_N'))dt \qquad 50'$$

The profit function is convex in wage cost. We assume that $\pi_w^C \leq 0$. By diminishing marginal productivity of labour, $w_N' \geq 0$.Thus, the product of the two terms on the right-hand side is negative and must be of a magnitude less than the wage rate (the first term in the expression) for the correct sign of the multiplier to go through. Pursuing the parallel procedure for the worker, the Hamiltonian is

$$H^W = v^W\big(N(t), k(N(t)), w(t)\big) + \mu(t)\left[(1+n)\left(\frac{k(N(t))}{1-w(t)}\right)\left\{g_{p_{ut}} + \left(1+\frac{1}{p_{ut}}\right)v_{ut}\right\}N(t)\right] \qquad 51'$$

Taking the derivative with respect to the wage,

$$N(t) = \mu(t)\left[(1+n)\left(\frac{k(N(t))}{[1-w(t)]^2}\right)\left\{g_{p_{ut}} + \left(1+\frac{1}{p_{ut}}\right)v_{ut}\right\}N(t)\right] \qquad 52'$$

Substituting this expression into the Hamiltonian, we get the maximized Hamiltonian for the worker.

$$H^{W*} = v^W\big(N(t), k(N(t)), w(t)\big) - N(t) \qquad 53'$$

The adjoint equation in this case is

$$\dot{\mu}(t) = r_w \mu(t) - H_N^{W*}$$

$$= r_w \mu(t) - w(t) - \upsilon_k^W (N(t), k(N(t), w(t)) k_N'(N(t)) + 1 \qquad 54'$$

The solution is

$$\mu(t) = e^{\int r_w(t)dt} \int e^{\int r_w(t)dt} (1 - w(t) - \upsilon_k^W k_N')dt \qquad 55'$$

Little can be said about the influence of capital intensity on utility and therefore the sign of υ_N^W. The term $k_N^{'}$ can also be signed any way but as long as its product with the attached term is 'small', the shadow price retains its natural sign.

The only mild comparison that can be made between the two solutions is through comparison of the pairs of equations 50 and 55 and 50′ and 55′. Even in a situation of conflict over the wage, in Nash equilibrium it must be 'high enough'. Recently, exploiting the Main Street-Wall Street metaphor more thoroughly, Thomas I. Palley, 2017, has made the case for wage-growth targeting respecting productivity changes as an adjunct to inflation targeting.

We now consider the second path to agrarian transformation and proceed to calculate first the open-loop Nash Equilibrium. We express difference equation 29 in state space form. Thus,

$$\dot{K}(t) = (1+n)(1+\varphi(t))K(t)$$

Using the definition $\dot{K}(t) - K(t) = I(t)$ where $I(t)$ is the flow of new investment, we rewrite the state equation as

$$\dot{K}(t) = [(1+n)(1+\varphi(t))]K(t) = K(t) + I(t)$$

This time a class of entrepreneurs who choose $\varphi(t)$ to maximize their inter temporal profits arises.

$$J^E = \int_0^T e^{-r_e t} \pi^E\big(K(t), I(t), \varphi(t)\big) dt \tag{44''}$$

Capitalists plan their investment to maximize

$$J^C = \int_0^T e^{-r_c t} \pi^C\big(K(t), I(t), \varphi(t)\big) dt \tag{45''}$$

It is not obvious, a priori, that the problem is a non-cooperative game. We build on this remark below.

Following the procedure above, the entrepreneurial Hamiltonian is

$$H^E = \pi^E\big(K(t), I(t), \varphi(t)\big) + \mu(t)\big[(1+n)\big(1+\varphi(t)\big)K(t)\big] \tag{46''}$$

Choosing the level of land-saving technical change to maximize the function,

$$\pi_\varphi^E\big(K(t), I(t), \varphi(t)\big) = \mu(t)(1+n)K(t) \tag{47''}$$

Putting this expression into the Hamiltonian, the maximized Hamiltonian is

$$H^{E*} = \pi^E\big(K(t), I(t), \varphi(t)\big) + \frac{\pi_\varphi^E\big(K(t), I(t), \varphi(t)\big)}{(1+n)K(t)}[K(t) + I(t)] \tag{48''}$$

The adjoint equation is

$$\dot{\mu}(t) = r_e \mu(t) - H_K^{E*}$$
$$= r_e \mu(t) - \pi_K^E + \frac{\pi_{\varphi K}^E[(1+n)K(t)] - (1+n)\pi_\varphi^E}{[(1+n)K(t)]^2}[K(t) + I(t)] - \frac{\pi_\varphi^E}{(1+n)K(t)}[(1+n)(1+\varphi(t)] \tag{49''}$$

The solution is

$$\mu(t) = e^{\int r_e(t)dt} \int e^{\int r_e(t)dt}\Big(-\pi_K^E + \frac{\pi_{\varphi K}^E[(1+n)K(t)] - (1+n)\pi_\varphi^E}{[(1+n)K(t)]^2}[K(t) + I(t)] -$$
$$\frac{\pi_\varphi^E}{(1+n)K(t)}[(1+n)(1+\varphi(t)])dt \tag{50''}$$

Duality theory is of little help with these behavioral responses. The responsibility of claiming an increase in the profits of the entrepreneur brought about by a unit relaxation of the constraint lies in the sign of $\pi^E_{\varphi K}$ being not just positive but strong enough to overpower the putative negative items in the expression and/or terms like π^E_K and π^E_φ being negative 'enough'. The case of the cross-order derivative being positive would suggest a 'strategic complementarity' between the two strategies. The positive first-order profit of the entrepreneur resulting from a change in the technological coefficients is increased by an increase in the stock of capital.

The capitalist Hamiltonian along Path 2 is

$$H^C = \pi^C\big(K(t), I(t), \varphi(t)\big) + \lambda(t)[K(t) + I(t)] \qquad 51''$$

The capitalist accumulates capital to maximize profits. We have

$$\pi^C_I(K(t), I(t), \varphi(t)) = -\lambda(t) \qquad 52''$$

With this expression in the Hamiltonian, the maximized Hamiltonian is

$$H^{C*} = \pi^C\big(K(t), I(t), \varphi(t)\big) - \pi^C_I\ [K(t) + I(t)] \qquad 53''$$

The adjoint equation is

$$\begin{aligned}\dot{\lambda}(t) &= r_c\lambda(t) - H^{C*}_K \\ &= r_c\lambda(t) - p_{ut} - \pi^C_{IK}[(1+n)(1+\varphi(t)]\end{aligned} \qquad 54''$$

The solution of this equation is

$$\lambda(t) = -e^{\int r_c(t)dt} \int e^{\int r_c(t)dt} \int\{p_{ut} + \pi^C_{IK}[(1+n)(1+\varphi(t)]\}dt \qquad 55''$$

We can build on the potential cooperative elements hinted at earlier. Assuming an initially constrained level of the capital stock, the restricted profit function of the capitalist is concave in the level of capital. With some latitude, we can then have $\pi_{IK}^{C} \leq 0$ and a positive shadow price of this constraint.

The next step is the calculation of the Markovian Nash Equilibrium of the game.

In the familiar manner, the entrepreneur optimizes her objective function on the assumption that the capitalist will deploy a feedback strategy, $I(K(t))$.

The Hamiltonian now is

$$H^E = \pi^E\left((K(t)), I(K(t)), \varphi(t)\right) + \mu(t)[K(t) + I(K(t)] \qquad 46'''$$

The first-order condition in the choice of land-using technical change is familiarly,

$$\pi_{\varphi}^{E}\big(K(t), I(K(t)), \varphi(t)\big) = \mu(t)(1+n)K(t) \qquad 47'''$$

Plugging this equation into the Hamiltonian, the maximized Hamiltonian is

$$H^{E*} = \pi^E\big(K(t), I(K(t)), \varphi(t)\big) + \frac{\pi_{\varphi}^{E}\big(K(t), I(K(t)), \varphi(t)\big)}{(1+n)K(t)}[K(t) + I(K(t)] \qquad 48'''$$

The adjoint equation is

$$\dot{\mu}(t) = r_e\mu(t) - H_K^{E*}$$

$$= r_e\mu(t) - \pi_K^E - \pi_I^E I'\big(K(t)\big) + \frac{\pi_{\varphi K}^{E}[(1+n)K(t)] + \pi_I^E I'(K(t)) - (1+n)\pi_{\varphi}^{E}}{[(1+n)K(t)]^2}[K(t) + I(K(t)] - \frac{\pi_{\varphi}^{E}}{(1+n)K(t)}[1 + I'(K(t))] \qquad 49'''$$

The solution is

$$\mu(t) = -e^{\int r_e(t)dt}\int e^{\int r_e(t)dt}\Big(\pi_K^E + \pi_I^E I' - \frac{\pi_{\varphi K}^{E}[(1+n)K(t)] + \pi_I^E I' - (1+n)\pi_{\varphi}^{E}}{[(1+n)K(t)]^2}[K(t) + I(K(t)] + \frac{\pi_{\varphi}^{E}}{(1+n)K(t)}[1 + I'(K(t))]\Big)dt \qquad 50'''$$

Our earlier remarks about responses of profit functions to changes in strategies and the state determining the sign of the shadow price on the left-hand side apply.

In like manner, the capitalist Hamiltonian is

$$H^C = \pi^C\left((K(t)), I(t), \varphi(K(t))\right) + \lambda(t)[K(t) + I(t)] \qquad 51'''$$

The first-order condition gives us

$$\pi_I^C(K(t), I(t), \varphi(K(t)) = -\lambda(t) \qquad 52'''$$

With this expression in the Hamiltonian, the maximized Hamiltonian is

$$H^{C*} = \pi^C(K(t), I(t), \varphi(K(t)) - \pi_I^C I(t) \qquad 53'''$$

The adjoint equation is

$$\dot{\lambda}(t) = r_c\lambda(t) - H_K^{C*}$$
$$= r_c\lambda(t) - p_{ut} - \pi_\varphi^C \varphi'_K + \pi_{IK}^C\{[(1+n)(1+\varphi)]\} + \pi_I^C[(1+n)(1+\varphi'_K)] \qquad 54'''$$

The solution of this differential equation is

$$\lambda(t) = -e^{\int r_c(t)dt} \int e^{\int r_c(t)dt}(p_{ut} + \pi_\varphi^C \varphi'_K - \pi_{IK}^C\{[(1+n)(1+\varphi)]\} +$$
$$\pi_I^C[(1+n)(1+\ \varphi'_K)]dt \qquad 55'''$$

Here too, our earlier remarks about the concavity of the profit function and the consequent positive left-hand side are carried over. A relaxation of the constraint benefits both protagonists. In other words, the increasing level of the capital stock benefits both capitalist and entrepreneur.

Usually models of class conflict in countries undergoing agricultural transformation comprise of three classes. We set up two games where combinations of two classes play a differential game. The first is a classical class conflict between capitalists and workers. Both are loggerheads over the wage. However, the solution is sustained only if the wage is 'high enough' in relation to other terms in the expressions. A Keynesian aggregation result might be at work here. While the wage is cost to the individual capitalist, it is income and demand for the system as whole. The second is one in which cooperative elements are suggested in the setup of the game. The capitalist chooses investment subject to the constraint of a state equation but the state equation is a capital accumulation equation. Although the entrepreneur chooses the level of technical change and is unconcerned about the level of investment, if both strategies are 'strategic complements', the accumulation of capital is welfare-enhancing for her as well. The tour through some history of thought it turns out is relevant. While the treatment is modern, the theme is old. The accumulation of capital and wages increasing in lockstep with equilibrium systemic relationships are the bases of growth and appropriate technical progress. Farmers may not adopt superior technologies like integrated pest management or move towards organic farming because they are locked into inferior outcomes (Balmann & Valentinov, 2016). Alternatively put, a given mode of production is the representation of historical events and avenues taken in previous epochs. Even within regions continuous with respect to climatic or social conditions, relations of production can differ vastly. Consequently, the provision of new technologies comes at a huge cost to providers who face the prospect of rejection by classes of farmers. For the same reason, moving a step backwards, R&D in agricultural research would suffer from chronic disincentives. Yet path dependence does not mean an inertial equilibrium for all time to come. Agriculture too has been transformed overnight by regime changes. Mazzucato's "entrepreneurial State" kicks the innovation ball at rest by dispelling the uncertainty that paralyses action. Both push and pull factors operate. Examples of the former are technical changes that pierce through the thick pall of centuries of inefficient practices. Illustrations of the latter are hostile environmental as well as class conditions that push small and marginal farmers towards the adoption of superior arrangements.

6.2 Das Finanzcapital

The title is intended to evoke the tussle in the composition of finance in the evolution of capitalism traced by Rudolf Hilferding in his time. Banks are added to the classic conflict between the two classes and we have a triumvirate, this time for advanced economies. Our class description follows the formulation set out in section 3.2. The following abbreviations will aid the presentation. Denote $\alpha \equiv 1 - \frac{r_{-1}^{l}}{CAR.BLR}$; $\beta \equiv \frac{\theta}{CAR.BLR}$. We subdivide the conflicts into three institutional configurations.

6.2.1 Banks and norms

The labour process is central to all non neoclassical accounts. For the purpose of the present section, the following connection with banking systems is sufficient. The limitations of universal suffrage in countries like Brazil, Mexico, and the US amplified the power of the elites and constricted the free development of banking institutions. A panel data set of eighteen of today's democracies over the 19th and 20th centuries refines the thesis (Degryse et al, 2013). The median voter is both investor and worker. If the distribution of the population is skewed towards the latter, there will be a bias towards labour and creditors and a central role will be played by creditor protection. Banks will be encouraged and will support debt holders. In contrast, if the majority weighs in the direction of investor protection, norms of stockholder protection will emerge in vibrant stock markets. The tradeoffs are familiar. Stock markets are risky but more profitable. Financial returns come at the cost of labour market development.

The next step is to describe the situation as a dynamic game. We adopt the formulation of Van Long (2010) and we present our system in continuous time. Thus, our state equation 31 becomes

$$\dot{L}(t) = \alpha L(t) + \frac{G(t)}{CAR.BLR} - \beta W(t)N(t)$$

Denoting ρ as her discount rate, the worker makes her work choices $N(t)$ so as to maximize her indirect utility function,

$$U_t = \int_0^\infty e^{-\rho t} u(N(t))dt \qquad 56$$

Assuming an identical degree of impatience, the business enterprise chooses its wage bill so as to optimize it profit function,

$$\Pi_t = \int_0^\infty e^{-\rho t} \pi\big(W(t)\big)dt \qquad 57$$

The open-loop Nash equilibrium (OLNE) is given by the following sets of conditions. In turn, the problem of the worker, taking the strategy of the manager $W^{OL}(t)$ as given, is solved as follows. With ψ as the co-state variable for the worker, her Hamiltonian function is

$$\mathcal{H} = u(N) + \psi\left(\alpha L + \frac{G}{CAR.BLR} - \beta W^{OL} N\right) \quad 58$$

The necessary conditions are

$$\frac{\partial \mathcal{H}}{\partial N} = u'(N) - \psi\beta W^{OL} = 0 \quad 59$$

$$-\dot{\psi} + \rho\psi = \frac{\partial \mathcal{H}}{\partial L} = \psi\alpha \quad 60$$

$$\dot{L} = \frac{\partial \mathcal{H}}{\partial \psi} = \left(\alpha L + \frac{G}{CAR.BLR} - \beta W^{OL} N\right) \quad 61$$

Hôtelling's lemma is $d\pi/dW = -N$. We can then write equation 59 as $\psi = \frac{u'(-\frac{d\pi}{dW^{OL}})}{\beta W^{OL}}$. The purpose is only to support our remarks made at the beginning of the section. In addition to β, the level of the costate variable is determined by the wage rate on offer.

We now compute the first-order conditions for the manager, taking the strategy, $N^{OL}(t)$, of the worker as given and with γ as the costate variable,

$$\mathcal{H} = \pi(W) + \gamma\left(\alpha L + \frac{G}{CAR.BLR} - \beta W N^{OL}\right) \quad 62$$

Taking the required derivatives,

$$\frac{\partial \mathcal{H}}{\partial W} = \pi'(W) - \gamma\beta N^{OL} = 0 \quad 63$$

$$-\dot{\gamma} + \rho\gamma = \frac{\partial \mathcal{H}}{\partial L} = \gamma\alpha \quad 64$$

$$\dot{L} = \frac{\partial \mathcal{H}}{\partial \gamma} = \left(\alpha L + \frac{G}{CAR.BLR} - \beta W N^{OL}\right) \quad 65$$

Hôtelling's lemma works cleanly here giving $\gamma = \frac{-1}{\beta}$.

In sum, an OLNE is a pair of functions (N^{OL}, W^{OL}) satisfying the following three differential equations.

$$\dot{\psi} = (\rho - \alpha)\psi. \qquad 66$$

$$\dot{\gamma} = (\rho - \alpha)\gamma \qquad 67$$

$$\dot{L} = \left(\alpha L + \frac{G}{CAR.BLR} - \beta W^{OL} N^{OL}\right) \qquad 68$$

The equations admit a steady-state solution $(\hat{\psi}, \hat{\gamma}, \hat{L})$, where

$$\hat{\psi} = \hat{\gamma} = \frac{\rho}{\alpha} \qquad 69$$

and$(1 - r^l)\hat{L} + G = \theta W^{Ol} N^{OL}$

The Jacobian matrix J of the system is

$$J = \begin{bmatrix} \rho - \alpha & 0 & 0 \\ 0 & \rho - \alpha & 0 \\ 0 & 0 & \alpha \end{bmatrix} \qquad 70$$

The condition for stability is that $\rho < \alpha$. To our discussion following stabilizing SFC norms in Section 3.3 we must add the preferences of members of the private sector as revealed in their discount rates. In the event of 'impatient' classes and 'low' interest rates, the authorities must step in with SFC norms to ensure that the inequality is met.

In the case of the Markov-perfect Nash equilibrium (MPNE), each player assumes that the other's strategy is a function of the state of the world, the level of loans, in the period. The maximand of the consumer remains equation 56 now subject to the dynamical equation

$$\dot{L}(t) = \alpha L(t) + \frac{G(t)}{CAR.BLR} - \beta W^{FB}(L(t))N(t)$$

Now the Hamiltonian is

$$\mathcal{H} = u(N) + \psi\left\{\alpha L + \frac{G}{CAR.BLR} - \beta W^{FB}(L)N\right\} \qquad 71$$

The necessary conditions this time are

$$\frac{\partial \mathcal{H}}{\partial N} = u'(N) - \psi\beta W^{FB} = 0 \qquad 72$$

$$-\dot{\psi} + \rho\psi = \frac{\partial \mathcal{H}}{\partial L} = \psi\left(\alpha - \beta\frac{dW^{FB}}{dL}N\right) \quad 73$$

$$\dot{L} = \frac{\partial \mathcal{H}}{\partial \psi} = \left\{\alpha L + \frac{G}{CAR.BLR} - \beta W^{FB}(L)N\right\} \quad 74$$

As expected, the difference between this set of equations and the earlier is that between 60 and 73, specifically the feedback element in the second term on the right-hand side of 73. Nothing can be said about the derivative, its sign and magnitude.

Coming to the entrepreneur, her Hamiltonian is

$$\mathcal{H} = \pi(W) + \gamma\left(\alpha L + \frac{G}{CAR.BLR} - \beta W N^{FB}(L)\right) \quad 75$$

In like manner, the first-order conditions for the entrepreneur are

$$\frac{\partial \mathcal{H}}{\partial W} = \pi'(W) - \gamma\beta N^{FB} = 0 \quad 76$$

$$-\dot{\gamma} + \rho\gamma = \frac{\partial \mathcal{H}}{\partial L} = \gamma\left(\alpha - \beta\frac{dN^{FB}}{dL}W\right) \quad 77$$

$$\dot{L} = \frac{\partial \mathcal{H}}{\partial \gamma} = \left(\alpha + \frac{G}{CAR.BLR} - \beta W N^{FB}\right) \quad 78$$

Again, economic theory provides little guidance about the derivative in 77. The MPNE is a pair of functions (N^{MP}, W^{MP}) satisfying the following three differential equations

$$\dot{\psi} = \left(\rho - \alpha - \beta\frac{dW^{FB}}{dL}N^{FP}\right)\psi \quad 79$$

$$\dot{\gamma} = \left(\rho - \alpha - \beta\frac{dN^{FB}}{dL}W^{FP}\right)\gamma \quad 80$$

$$\dot{L} = \left(\alpha L + \frac{G}{CAR.\rho} - \beta W^{FP}N^{FP}\right) \quad 81$$

The steady-state $(\hat{\psi}, \hat{\gamma}, \hat{L})$ is given by

$$\hat{\psi} = \frac{\rho-\alpha}{\beta.\frac{dW^{FB}}{dL}} \text{and } \hat{\gamma} = \frac{\rho-\alpha}{\beta.\frac{dN^{FB}}{dL}} \quad 82$$

and, as earlier $(1 - r^l)\hat{L} + G = \theta W^{FP} N^{FP}$.

It is time to install built-in stabilizers. Equations 79 and 80 suggest the following policy regime whose counter cyclicality will be confirmed below.

$$\beta = max\left(\frac{1}{\frac{dW^{FB}}{dL}N^{MP}}, \frac{1}{\frac{dN^{FB}}{dL}W^{FB}}\right)$$

For the sake of simplicity in our statement of stability we take the other expression in the bracket as unity in our Jacobian.

The Jacobian matrix J of the system is

$$J = \begin{bmatrix} \rho - \alpha - 1 & 0 & 0 \\ 0 & \rho - \alpha - 1 & 0 \\ 0 & 0 & \alpha \end{bmatrix} \qquad 83$$

Since the matrix varies slightly from equation 70, the remarks concerning stability transfer. The slight amendment to the requirement now is that $\rho - 1 < \alpha$. The case for countercyclical capital requirements (CRRs) can be traced to Minsky (Greenwood-Nimmo & Tarassow, 2013). Quantity constraints on lending in booms protect the portfolios of banks from large contractions in the value of collateral assets. The central bank should refine capital requirements so that the balance sheets of financial institutions are not impaired. In short, entrepreneurs and banks are the chief protagonists here and the latter can create credit subject to prudential constraints in response to the plans of the former (Scarano, 2013). The macroeconomic and inter temporal constraint according to which credit might be constrained by liquidity must be faced. 'Production credit' is the absence of consumption, the transference of savings from households to banks. It is 'monetary capital' in search of investment outlets. 'Capital credit' is the transformation of idle hoards in banks into 'active monetary capital'. The largest part will be amortization funds, not modelled here. The rest with capitalists alongside entrepreneurs will consist of actual saving. A recent study of 130 recessions in 26 capitalist economies over five decades confirms that rapid credit growth immediately prior to a recession predicts a longer-lasting downturn than when credit growth has been steady (Bridges et al, 2017). The metrics of the prolonged downturns include severe impairment of employment and productivity.

The section can be summarised in the following proposition: Stability of bank-led regimes is ensured by calibrated capital adequacy ratios and bank liquidity ratios and the income tax rate. The values of these numbers are derived along with other structural variables and can, therefore, vary from system to system. Secondly, the law of one price in borrowing and lending may or may not hold. Only a lower bound on the loan rate of interest is suggested by our model.

6.2.2 Stock markets and 'financialization'

Equation 32 reproduced below is accorded pride of place in the instance of the present subsection.

$$C + \Delta e p_e + G = WN + p_e e_{-1} / PE$$

Divide the expression by p_e and in an abuse of notation we use the same variables above, now expressed in 'real' terms, that is deflated by the equity price index. The move might not be without merit for a complaint against standard practice is that while commodity price inflation occupies attention, little note is made of asset prices.

In continuous time, we have

$$\dot{e}(t) = (1 + \frac{1}{PE})e(t) + W(t)N(t) - C(t) - G(t)$$

This time, the substantive economics of the problem indicates that it is the consumer incarnation of the representative agent that is at play. So 56 is transformed to the problem of choosing $C(t)$ to maximize her direct utility function

$$U_t = \int_0^\infty e^{-\rho t} u(C(t)) dt \qquad 56'$$

We retain the maximand of the business enterprise. Reproducing equation 57, the business enterprise chooses its wage bill $W(t)$ so as to optimize it profit function

$$\Pi_t = \int_0^\infty e^{-\rho t}\pi(W(t))dt \qquad 57'$$

Once again, the OLNE is given by the following sets of conditions. The equations for the consumer, taking the strategy $W^{OL}(t)$ of the business executive as given, follow. Her Hamiltonian, taking ψ as her co-state variable is

$$\mathcal{H} = u(C) + \psi\left\{(1 + \tfrac{1}{PE})e + W^{OL}N - C - G)\right\} \qquad 58'$$

The first-order conditions are

$$\frac{\partial \mathcal{H}}{\partial C} = u'(C) - \psi = 0 \qquad 59'$$

$$-\dot{\psi} + \rho\psi = \frac{\partial \mathcal{H}}{\partial e} = \psi\left(1 + \tfrac{1}{PE}\right) \qquad 60'$$

$$\dot{e} = \frac{\partial \mathcal{H}}{\partial \psi} = \left\{(1 + \tfrac{1}{PE})e + W^{OL}N - C - G\right\} \qquad 61'$$

Denote $-\frac{U''(C)C}{U'(C)}$ the elasticity of intertemporal substitution of consumption by φ.

Combining equations 59′ and 60′, we get

$$\dot{C} = \frac{1}{\varphi}\left\{\rho - (1 + \frac{1}{PE})\right\}C$$

Following in earlier tracks, we now compute the first-order conditions for the manager, taking the strategy $C^{OL}(t)$ of the consumer as given and with γ as the costate variable.

$$\mathcal{H} = \pi(W) + \gamma\left\{(1 + \tfrac{1}{PE})e + WN - C^{OL} - G)\right\} \qquad 62'$$

Taking the required derivatives

$$\frac{\partial \mathcal{H}}{\partial W} = \pi'(W) + \gamma N = 0 \qquad 63'$$

$$-\dot{\gamma} + \rho\gamma = \frac{\partial \mathcal{H}}{\partial e} = \gamma\left(1 + \frac{1}{PE}\right) \qquad 64'$$

$$\dot{e} = \frac{\partial \mathcal{H}}{\partial \gamma} = \left\{(1 + \frac{1}{PE})e + WN - C^{OL} - G)\right\} \qquad 65'$$

Hôtelling's lemma, yet again, in 63′ gives the value of gamma as unity. Equation 64′ in that case turns out to be $\rho = 1 + \frac{1}{PE}$. The differential equation for consumption above vanishes when this expression is substituted in it.

Thus, an OLNE is a pair (C^{OL}, N^{OL}) satisfying the single differential equation,

$$\dot{e} = \left\{(1 + \frac{1}{PE})e + WN^{OL} - C^{OL} - G)\right\} \qquad 66'$$

The steady-state solution $\hat{e}$ is given by

$$C^{OL} + G = \rho\hat{e} + WN^{OL} \qquad 69'$$

The requirement for stability is

$$\left(1 + \frac{1}{PE}\right) < 1 \text{or} \ \rho < 1. \qquad 70'$$

Once more, when we introduce agents their discount rates must be added to the requirements for stability of the previous section derived only in terms of structural coefficients. The loud and clear message is that the patience of workers and capitalists must dovetail with the requirements of manufacturing and real activity as a counter to financialization.

Turning now to the MPNE, the consumer takes the feedback strategy of the firm W^{FB} as given. The constraint she confronts now is

$$\dot{e}(t) = (1 + \frac{1}{PE})e(t) + W^{FB}(e(t))N^{FB}(t) - C(t) - G(t)$$

Her Hamiltonian is

$$\mathcal{H} = u(C) + \psi\left\{(1 + \tfrac{1}{PE})e + W^{FB}(e)N - C - G)\right\} \tag{71'}$$

The familiar necessary conditions are

$$\frac{\partial \mathcal{H}}{\partial C} = u'(C) - \psi = 0 \tag{72'}$$

$$-\dot{\psi} + \rho\psi = \frac{\partial \mathcal{H}}{\partial e} = \psi\left\{\left(1 + \tfrac{1}{PE}\right) + N\frac{dW^{FB}}{de}\right\} \tag{73'}$$

$$\dot{e} = \frac{\partial \mathcal{H}}{\partial \psi} = \left\{(1 + \tfrac{1}{PE})e + W^{FB}N - C - G\right\} \tag{74'}$$

As in the previous steps, we can combine equations to give a differential equation in consumption rather than the costate variable,

$$\dot{C} = \frac{1}{\varphi}\left\{\rho - \left(1 + \frac{1}{PE}\right) - N\frac{dW^{FB}}{de}\right\}C$$

The next step is to compute the first-order conditions for the manager, taking the strategy $C^{FB}(e(t))$ of the consumer as given and with γ as the costate variable. The Hamiltonian now is

$$\mathcal{H} = \pi(W) + \gamma\left\{(1 + \tfrac{1}{PE})e + WN - C^{FB}(e) - G)\right\} \tag{75'}$$

Taking the required derivatives

$$\frac{\partial \mathcal{H}}{\partial W} = \pi'(W) + \gamma N = 0 \tag{76'}$$

$$-\dot{\gamma} + \rho\gamma = \frac{\partial \mathcal{H}}{\partial e} = \gamma\left\{\left(1 + \tfrac{1}{PE}\right) - \frac{dC^{FB}}{de}\right\} \tag{77'}$$

$$\dot{e} = \frac{\partial \mathcal{H}}{\partial \gamma} = \left\{(1 + \tfrac{1}{PE})e + WN - C^{FB} - G)\right\} \tag{78'}$$

Once more, Hôtelling's lemma gives $\gamma = 1$ in 76′ and 77′ then simplifies to $\left(1 + \frac{1}{PE}\right) = \rho + \frac{dC^{FB}}{de}$.

Thus, the MPNE is the strategy pair (C^{FB}, W^{FB}) satisfying the following equations

$$\dot{C^{FB}} = \frac{1}{\varphi}\left\{-\frac{dC^{FB}}{de} - N\frac{dW^{FB}}{de}\right\}C^{FB} \quad 79'$$

$$\dot{e} = \left\{\rho + \frac{dC^{FB}}{de}\right\}e + W^{FB}N - C^{FB} - G \quad 80'$$

For the steady-state of the system,

$$0 = \frac{1}{\varphi}\left\{-\frac{dC^{FB}}{de} - N\frac{dW^{FB}}{de}\right\}C^{FB} \quad 81'$$

$$\widehat{C^{FB}} + G = (\rho + \frac{dC^{FB}}{de})\hat{e} + W^{FB}N \quad 82'$$

A condition that must be met is $\frac{dW^{FB}}{de} \leq 0$. The requirement is part of the description of "financialization". The regime includes attracting human resources into the financial churning industry and the corresponding withdrawal of labour from manufacturing and agriculture. Wage income (and consumption) falls and rentier income (and consumption) increases. The labour force participation rate in the US has been falling since 2000 (Dantas & Wray, 2017). Especially for the prime-age working cohort, the reasons continue to be effective demand failures, an empty set of job-creating projects, and stagnant wages. Short-term spikes in activity have been driven by asset-price bubbles that provide quick fixes to rentiers and nothing to workers.

The Jacobian of the system is

$$J = \begin{bmatrix} \frac{1}{\varphi}\left\{-\frac{dC^{FB}}{de} - N\frac{dW^{FB}}{de}\right\} & 0 \\ 0 & \rho + \frac{dC^{FB}}{de} \end{bmatrix} \quad 83'$$

Clearly, the feedback behaviour is critical. Both the responses of wages and consumption to the stock of shares cannot be arbitrarily high. However, the high elasticity of response is precisely what underlies the group behaviour of Minsky's model. He observed over many financial-real cycles a move from open-loop to closed-loop behaviour. As the good times roll on, the response of wages and consumption to the stock market boom might be in excess of one-to-one. Empirically, through the "great moderation" in the US the graph of wages was sloping upward slightly at best. There is a procyclical, self-referential feedback loop between individual behaviour and the state of the economy (Solomon & Golo, 2014). Secondly, under what has been called "patrimonial capitalism" the consumption derivative in absolute terms cannot be regarded as higher than the wage derivative with respect to holdings of equities along traditional class lines (Milanovic, 2013). However, property has penetrated decisively into the middle and working classes. The top 1% of the wealth pyramid consists of "coupon-clipping rentiers" as well as the "working rich". The well-known condition on the determinant leads to the requirement $N\frac{dW^{FB}}{de} > \frac{dC^{FB}}{de}$. The product of the behavioural response on the left-hand side with the number of people employed should meet the condition easily.

The Jacobian suggests a nonlinear underlying transformation. The stability conditions need to be refined to the following (Medio & Lines, 2001)

$$1 + trJ + detJ > 0 \quad \text{a}$$

$$1 - trJ + detJ > 0 \quad \text{b}$$

$$1 - detJ > 0 \quad \text{c}$$

In the case of inequality b being an equality, the other conditions holding, the outcome is a fold bifurcation. In our case, a *fold bifurcation* results when

$$\text{Either } \left\{-\frac{dC^{FB}}{de} - N\frac{dW^{FB}}{de}\right\} = \varphi \text{ or } \rho + \frac{dC^{FB}}{de} = 1$$

A Neimark-Sacker bifurcation is the outcome when condition c is an equality. That is, a *Neimark-Sacker bifurcation* results in our model when

$$\left\{-\frac{dC^{FB}}{de} - N\frac{dW^{FB}}{de}\right\}\left\{\rho + \frac{dC^{FB}}{de}\right\} = \varphi$$

To summarise, we translate Hyman Minsky's "financial instability hypothesis" of section 2.2 for a "financialized" economy: open-loop strategies will at first support "hedge" funding of positions. As the cycle gathers momentum, optimism gives way to closed-loop strategies leading to "speculative" and then "Ponzi" financing or the transformation of workers to rentiers which may destabilising.

6.2.3 The government bond and money

Our final treatment of the micro foundations of G&L macroeconomics is the third regime of Sections 3.2 and 3.3. Once more we reproduce the discrete equation as a reminder.

$$\triangle BL \triangle p_{\mathrm{bL}} = YD_{\mathrm{HS}} - C - I$$

A state-space representation is

$$\dot{BL}(t)\dot{p_{bL}}(t) = BL(t)p_{bL(t)} + YD_{HS}(t) - C(t) - I(t)$$

Yet again, the dynamical constraints suggest the representative agent. Thus, the consumer chooses $C(t)$ to maximize

$$U_t = \int_0^{\infty} e^{-\rho t} u(C(t))dt \qquad 56''$$

Since investment is the accumulation of capital, $I \equiv K - K_{-1}$, the purchase executive has to choose the stock of capital in the current period. Her objective function is

$$\Pi_t = \int_0^{\infty} e^{-\rho t} \pi(K(t))dt \qquad 57''$$

For the penultimate time, the solution of the following equations gives the OLNE. The equations for the consumer, taking the strategy $K^{OL}(t)$ of the entrepreneur as given, follow. Her Hamiltonian, taking ψ as her co-state variable is

$$\mathcal{H} = u(C) + \psi(BLp_{bL} + YD_{HS} - C - K^{OL} + K) \qquad 58''$$

The necessary conditions are

$$\frac{\partial \mathcal{H}}{\partial C} = u'(C) - \psi = 0 \qquad 59''$$

$$-\dot{\psi} + \rho\psi = \frac{\partial \mathcal{H}}{\partial BLp_{bL}} = \psi \qquad 60''$$

$$\dot{BLp_{bL}} = \frac{\partial \mathcal{H}}{\partial \gamma} = (BLp_{bL} + YD_{HS} - C - K^{OL}) \qquad 61''$$

Combining 59″ and 60″,

$$\dot{C} = \frac{\rho - 1}{\varphi} C$$

In the familiar manner, we now compute the first-order conditions for the manager, taking the strategy $C^{OL}(t)$ of the consumer as given and with γ as the costate variable.

$$\mathcal{H} = \pi(K) + \gamma(BLp_{bL} + YD_{HS} - C^{OL} - K) \qquad 62''$$

Taking the required derivatives,

$$\frac{\partial \mathcal{H}}{\partial K} = \pi'(K) - \gamma = 0 \qquad 63''$$

$$-\dot{\gamma} + \rho\gamma = \frac{\partial \mathcal{H}}{\partial BLp_{bL}} = \gamma \qquad 64''$$

$$\dot{BLp_{bL}} = \frac{\partial \mathcal{H}}{\partial \gamma} = (BLp_{bL} + YD_{HS} - C^{OL} - K) \qquad 65''$$

We call$-\frac{\pi''(K)K}{\pi'(K)}$ the elasticity of intertemporal substitution of production and denote it by τ. If we regard the profit function as restricted in the level of capital, then the function is strictly concave in capital. This brings a welcome symmetry with the comparable concept used in the case of the consumer.

Equations 63″ and 64″ give us

$$\dot{K} = \frac{\rho - 1}{\tau} K$$

Consequently, the OLNE is a pair (C^{OL}, K^{OL}) satisfying the following three equations

$$\dot{C^{OL}} = \frac{\rho-1}{\varphi} C^{OL} \qquad 66''$$

$$\dot{K^{OL}} = \frac{\rho-1}{\tau} K^{OL} \qquad 67''$$

$$\dot{BL}\dot{p_{bL}} = BLp_{bL} + YD_{HS} - C^{Ol} - K^{OL} \qquad 68''$$

We proceed to examine the steady-state properties. The single discount rate is clearly a restriction here. We must have different degrees of impatience for the players, a ρ stays for the consumer and the discount rate for the producer is µ. In that case, the steady state $\left(\widehat{C^{OL}}, \widehat{K^{Ol}}, \widehat{BL}\widehat{p_{bL}}\right)$ is

$$\rho = \frac{1}{\varphi}\text{and } \mu = \frac{1}{\tau} \text{ and } \widehat{BL}\widehat{p_{bL}} + YD_{HS} = \widehat{C^{OL}} + \widehat{K^{OL}} \qquad 69''$$

Stability is established by the Jacobian

$$J = \begin{bmatrix} \frac{\rho-1}{\varphi} & 0 & 0 \\ 0 & \frac{\mu-1}{\tau} & 0 \\ -1 & -1 & 1 \end{bmatrix} \qquad 70''$$

The conditions for stability are unlike in the earlier cases without any bounds needing to be imposed on the elements of the matrix. Discount rates are, by definition, less than unity. In sum, only fundamental consumption and production parameters matter in an economy in which the government bond is equivalent to money.

In the case of closed-loop strategies, the consumer takes the feedback strategy of the investor $K^{FB}(BLp_{bL}(t))$ as given. She confronts the state evolution equation

$$\dot{BL(t)}\dot{p_{bL}(t)} = BL(t)p_{bL(t)} + YD_{HS}(t) - C(t) - K^{FB}\left(BLp_{bL}(t)\right)$$

Turning to the MPNE, the consumer's Hamiltonian taking ψ as her co-state variable is

$$\mathcal{H} = u(C) + \psi(BLp_{bL} + YD_{HS} - C - K^{FB}(BLp_{bL}) + K) \qquad 71''$$

The necessary conditions are

$$\frac{\partial \mathcal{H}}{\partial C} = u'(C) - \psi = 0 \qquad 72''$$

$$-\dot{\psi} + \rho\psi = \frac{\partial \mathcal{H}}{\partial BLp_{bL}} = \psi\left(1 - \frac{dK^{FB}}{dBLp_{bL}}\right) \qquad 73''$$

$$\dot{BLp_{bL}} = \frac{\partial \mathcal{H}}{\partial \gamma} = (BLp_{bL} + YD_{HS} - C - K^{OL}) \qquad 74''$$

Combining 73″ and 74″ to eliminate the costate variable,

$$\dot{C} = \frac{1}{\varphi}\left\{\rho - 1 + \frac{dK^{FB}}{dBLp_{bL}}\right\}C$$

The next step is to compute the first-order conditions for the manager taking the strategy $C^{FB}(e(t))$ of the consumer as given and with γ as the costate variable. The Hamiltonian now is

$$\mathcal{H} = \pi(K) + \gamma(BLp_{bL} + YD_{HS} - C^{FB}(BLp_{bL}) - K) \qquad 75''$$

Taking the required derivatives

$$\frac{\partial \mathcal{H}}{\partial K} = \pi'(K) - \gamma = 0 \qquad 76''$$

$$-\dot{\gamma} + \mu\gamma = \frac{\partial \mathcal{H}}{\partial BLp_{bL}} = \gamma\left(1 - \frac{dC^{FB}}{dBLp_{bL}}\right) \qquad 77''$$

$$\dot{BLp_{bL}} = \frac{\partial \mathcal{H}}{\partial \gamma} = (BLp_{bL} + YD_{HS} - C^{FB} - K) \qquad 78''$$

Equations 76″ and 77″ deliver

$$\dot{K} = \frac{1}{\tau}\left(\mu - 1 + \frac{dC^{FB}}{dBLp_{bL}}\right)K$$

Therefore, the MPNE is a pair of strategies (C^{FB}, K^{FB}) satisfying

$$\dot{C^{FB}} = \frac{1}{\varphi}\left\{\rho - 1 + \frac{dK}{dBLp_{bL}}\right\} C^{FB} \quad 79''$$

$$\dot{K^{FB}} = \frac{1}{\tau}\left(\mu - 1 + \frac{dC}{dBLp_{bL}}\right) K^{FB} \quad 80''$$

$$\dot{BLp_{bL}} = (BLp_{bL} + YD_{HS} - C^{FB} - K^{FB}) \quad 81''$$

The steady state $\left(\hat{C}, \hat{K}, \widehat{BL}\widehat{p_{bL}}\right)$ is given by

$$\rho + \frac{d\widehat{K^{FB}}}{d\widehat{Bl}\widehat{p_{bL}}} = 1;\ \mu + \frac{d\widehat{C^{FB}}}{d\widehat{BL}\widehat{p_{bL}}} = 1;\ \widehat{BL}\widehat{p_{bL}} + YD_{HS} = \widehat{C^{FB}} + \widehat{K^{FB}} \quad 82''$$

The Jacobian is

$$J = \begin{bmatrix} \frac{\rho - 1 + \frac{dK^{FB}}{dBLp_{bL}}}{\varphi} & 0 & 0 \\ 0 & \frac{\mu - 1 + \frac{dC^{FB}}{dBLp_{bL}}}{\tau} & 0 \\ -1 & -1 & 1 \end{bmatrix} \quad 83''$$

The derivatives are a discussion point. Assuming that they are positive, the case for stability must be $\frac{dK^{FB}}{dBLp_{bL}} < \rho$ and $\frac{dC^{FB}}{dBLp_{bL}} < \mu$. One recourse is the Folk Theorem. Simply assume that the players are patient enough so that the right-hand side of both inequalities is sufficiently high. Coming to the left-hand sides, the first derivative is likely to negligible if has a value at all. There is nothing in the model to suggest an impact of the value of bonds on the capital stock. On the other hand, the other derivative is the wealth effect on the rentier which might be high. In section 7.2, we introduce the surgical tools of the fiscal authorities who enter to euthanize the rentier. Thereby they act in concert with the central bank in fulfilling the mandate of financial stability and monetary policy. Minsky pointed out that the information sets involved in both tasks are common (Esen & Binati, 2013). Primarily, central banks are expected to ensure the smooth functioning of the payments system so that all economic entities can meet what Minsky called their survival constraints (see also Laidler, 2013). As a consequence, ever since Henry Thornton at least the Lender of Last Resort function of central banks has been pivotal.

Grubb is vindicated once again. The government bond is identical to fiat money. Other things being equal, the institution supports the behaviour of heterogeneous agents as they go about their business of consuming and working and producing. Only rentier responses are a cause for concern.

We have inverted standard practice dictated by general equilibrium and new Keynesian economics and explored the dynamical constraints faced by agents over time first, thereafter turning to their preferences. Always at the back of the mind of the macroeconomic theorist are the phases of the cycle. The cycle feeds back into agent behaviour and the latter by their responses heighten the fluctuations. Risk characteristics of individuals are not given. However, as classes, predilections move from risk aversion to risk love as activity turns from depression to golden ages. Thus, economies driven by stock market behaviour are susceptible to crises and breakdown. Consequently, in the aftermath of the last major financial meltdown in the US, attention is focussed on strengthening the banking system. Both international norms are sought and traditional fiscal instruments are being polished. In our steady states, not just government expenditure but income taxes enter as stabilising coefficients. The model could be extended to include indirect taxes and taxes on wealth. The short message is that both macroeconomic organs of the government should coordinate to create jobs at a decent wage relative to earnings from stocks and shares.

Chapter 7

Restoring a monetary production system

We approach the destination of our return journey from the phantasmagoria of finance to the real world begun in Chapter 4. Our macro foundations of micro economics strategy culminates in exercises showing as earlier that 'positive' and 'normative' are one. The monetary policy instrument that comes first, the fiscal weapons that follow, as well as the opening of the closed economy we conclude with, consist of variables and relationships every student of economics is familiar with. In our hands, however, they assume new forms.

7.1 Opening the Discount Window

Every student is taught that the discount window opens to a detention room in a central bank where erring bank managers who cannot meet statutory liquidity requirements are scolded, only to be forgiven at the price of a penal rate of interest. The stain of a bad reputation is not easy to rub off and partly explains the accumulation of idle reserves in banks even beyond national and Basel norms. In contrast, we dig into the history of central banks, not excluding the history of the Fed, to unearth and model the market for bankers' acceptances (Gorton, 2013). In the spirit of the Real Bills Doctrine, central bank participation in the bills market created "elastic currency". Rediscounting allowed banks to exchange private debt for currency. The Federal Reserve Act of 1913 allowed for the district Federal Reserve Banks to operate discount windows with perfectly elastic demand schedules at the posted discount rate (Leeper & Nason, 2014). Private banks expected that the commercial paper brought to the discount window would be accepted by the Federal Reserve Bank but discounted at the posted rate. The commitment rested on the assumption that the discount rate in excess of the rates on commercial paper would induce banks to minimize the securities presented at the discount window. A brake would be imposed on credit granted for speculative purposes in the view of the Fed.

Coming to the present, there is the suggestion that Too Big To Fail (TBTF) financial institutions should be broken up into independent parts (Fisher, 2013). Only the commercial banking segment would benefit from deposit insurance and the discount window. The discount window can be a sophisticated weapon in the armory of CBs to unfreeze risk-averse bankers (Greider, 2013). In addition, it could underpin special vehicles to direct lending to credit-starved sectors like small business. It could influence the propensity to invest by backstopping private-public bonds needed to overhaul crumbling public assets. The expectation is that in future systemic liquidity provision will embrace three elements: 1. standing lending facilities that are free of stigma, 2. regular provision of loan funding, and 3. a menu of acceptable collateral (Domanski et al, 2014). We connect with modern translations of the Currency School versus Banking School debate (Lainà, 2015; Goodhart & Jensen, 2015). Thus, Full-Reserve Banking might halt bank runs but does not address the other primary function of a bank, to fund the capital development of an economy. The main problem for the Currency School was operation with a strict distinction between 'money' and 'near-money'. The Banking School, in contrast, worked with a spectrum of liquid assets. There was no clear dividing line between monetary assets and quasi-money assets. The money stock was endogenous. Causation ran from the economy to money and vice versa and the key link between the two was credit creation. The following sequence could be traced. The central bank sets an interest rate so as to achieve some target and then meets the legitimate demands by commercial banks for reserves at that rate. The monetary base becomes endogenous and the money multiplier works in reverse to determine high-powered money. In like manner, given the central bank rate commercial banks must set the terms and conditions for lending and meet the legitimate demand for credit by borrowers satisfying these criteria. A central requirement for the Banking School is that the profile of an intermediary's assets should match its liabilities. If, for instance, liabilities are short-term and of fixed value, assets should be liquid as well, subject to little price variation with adequate equity support to meet any untoward collapse in asset prices. The unfortunate fact is that the banking sector has roundly departed from Banking School precepts. All over, the banking sector is making long-term, illiquid, property-related, mortgage loans to individuals and on commercial real estate. Banks' liquid assets are run down on the supposition that necessary cash is always available in wholesale markets.

All the notations and definitions below are taken from G&L. Commercial banks will hold a sufficient amount of bills to absorb fluctuations in money deposits M or loans L. Despite the best of intentions, however, the stock of bills held might drop precipitously. The buffer, under such circumstances, is provided by advances A supplied by the central bank at a price r_a. G&L (2007, p 337) provide a subtle account of thresholds below which an advances demand function will operate. However, keeping our focus in mind we dispense with bill holding and cut to advances defining a *net bank liquidity ratio* as A/M. The *capital adequacy ratio*, $CAR = M/L$. Taking the product of the two ratios introduced, $BLR.CAR = A/L$. Call this variable LA (loans & advances). By definition, $A_t = (1 + r_{at-1})A_{t-1}$ and with r_l the loan rate, $L_t = (1 + r_{lt-1})L_{t-1}$. Taking the ratio of the two equations and resorting to continuous time in the notations of Dockner, Jørgensen, Van Long & Sorger, 2000, we have the following state equation,

$$\dot{LA}(t) = [r_a(t) - r_l(t)]LA(t), LA(0) = LA_0 \qquad \text{a}$$

The central bank's choice variable is the rate of interest on its advances, the control variable of the commercial bank the loan rate. In that case, each player i seeks to maximize its total payoff over the planning horizon at the discount rate $r_i \geq 0$,

$$J^i = \int_0^T e^{-r_i t}\pi^i(LA(t), r_a(t), r_l(t))dt \qquad 84$$

We will solve for the equilibria of the game. The frosted-glass discount window metaphor is used to describe the raising of the window high enough to scrutinize the quality of the collateral without the identity of the discounter being revealed. Gorton & Ordoñez (2014) add secrecy to Bagehot's rule. However, Flandreau and Ugolini (2014) favour non-anonymous central bank lending. In the language of differential games, not raising the window at all would correspond to the open-loop Nash equilibrium while perfect information about collateral is the closed-loop Nash equilibrium.

There is no inflation-unemployment tradeoff to define a central bank payoff function. At this primary level of accounting, it stands for a representative depositor utility function. In theory, supply of deposits D would equal demand for deposits at a market-clearing price r_d. The supply of loans equals the demand for loans and deposits equal loans in equilibrium. Plugging in D instead of A in our differential equation, the dynamics becomes trivial. At the same time, the null rate(s) of interest of pure Ramsey theory are thrown up. Accordingly, we will exploit the envelope theorem and duality theory in the case of central bank optimization exercises. Making explicit the supply of deposits and the demand for loans in the individual utility functions, we have in the case of the central bank $\pi^{CB}(D(t), L(t), r_d(t), r_l(t))$. With the value of the other variables given at their optimal levels, the derivative of the indirect utility function with respect to the deposit rate gives the demand function for deposits $\pi^{CB}_{r_a}(D(t), L(t), r_d(t), r_l(t)) = D(t)$. In like manner, the price of deposits being exogenous and other variables being parametric at their optimal levels, the derivative of the Lagrangian with respect to the quantity of deposits gives $\pi_D^{CB}(D(t), L(t), r_d(t), r_l(t)) = r_d$. Similar derivations apply in the case of the bank. We proceed to calculate the equilibria of the game.

The open-loop Nash Equilibrium is derived as follows.

The central bank Hamiltonian is

$$H^{CB}(LA(t), r_a(t), r_l(t)) = \pi^{CB}(LA(t), r_a(t), r_l(t)) + \lambda(t)\{[r_a(t) - r_l(t)]LA(t)\} \qquad 85$$

Maximizing with respect to the deposit rate,

$$\lambda(t)LA(t) = -D(t) \qquad 86$$

Substituting this expression into the Hamiltonian, the maximized Hamiltonian is

$$H^{CB*} = \pi^{CB}(LA(t), r_a(t), r_l(t)) - \frac{[r_a(t) - r_l(t)]}{LA(t)} D(t) \qquad 87$$

Note that we have used central bank advances as a proxy for deposits in applying duality theory.

The adjoint equation is

$$\dot{\lambda}(t) = r_a\lambda(t) - H_{LA}^{CB*} = r_a\lambda(t) - r_a + \frac{r_a - r_l}{LA^2} \qquad 88$$

Once more, we have used the shortcut $\pi_{LA}^{CB}(LA(t), r_a(t), r_l(t)) = \pi_D^{CB}(D(t), L(t), r_d(t), r_l(t)) = r_d = r_a$ with all the caveats mentioned. The solution to the equation is

$$\lambda(t) = -e^{\int r_a(t)dt} \int e^{\int r_a(t)} \left[r_a(t) + \frac{r_a(t) - r_l(t)}{LA(t)^2}\right] dt \qquad 89$$

Thus, the optimal control for the central bank is given by the equation using 86,

$$\{e^{\int r_a(t)dt} \int e^{\int r_a(t)} \left[r_a(t) - \frac{r_a(t)-r_l(t)}{LA(t)^2}\right] dt\}LA(t) = D(t) \quad 90$$

Coming to the bank, its Hamiltonian is

$$H^B(LA(t), r_a(t), r_l(t)) = \pi^B(LA(t), r_a(t), r_l(t)) + \mu(t)\{[r_a(t) - r_l(t)]LA(t)\} \quad 91$$

The open-loop strategy for the bank is

$$\mu(t)LA(t) = -L(t) \quad 92$$

In this case, Hôtelling's lemma, $\pi^B_{r_l} = -L(t)$, applies.

The maximized Hamiltonian turns out to be

$$H^{B*} = \pi^B(LA(t), r_a(t), r_l(t)) - L(t)\{[r_a(t) - r_l(t)]LA(t)\} \quad 93$$

Using $\pi^B_{LA}(LA(t), r_a(t), r_l(t)) = \pi^B_L(D(t), L(t), r_d(t), r_l(t)) = r_l(t)$, the adjoint equation is

$$\dot{\mu}(t) = r_l\mu(t) - r_l + L(t)[r_a(t) - r_l(t)] \quad 94$$

The solution is

$$\mu(t) = -e^{\int r_l(t)dt} \int e^{\int r_l(t)} [r_l - L(t)[r_a(t) - r_l(t)]]dt \quad 95$$

Consequently, the optimal bank strategy is given implicitly by

$$\{e^{\int r_l(t)dt} \int e^{\int r_l(t)} [r_l - L(t)[r_a(t) - r_l(t)]]dt\}LA(t) = L(t) \quad 96$$

Now, take the ratio of 90 to 96. The purpose is to capitalize on the assumption that $A/L = LA = D/L$. Substitute in equation a and we have

$$\dot{LA}(t) = [r_a(t) - r_l(t)]\left[e^{\int (r_a(t)-r_l(t)dt} \int e^{\int (r_a(t)-r_l(t)} \frac{r_a(t) - \frac{r_a(t)-r_l(t)}{LA(t)^2}}{r_l(t) - L(t)[r_a(t) - r_l(t)]} dt\right] \qquad 97$$

This first-order equation has an equilibrium point at $LA(t) = 0$ when $r_a(t) - r_l(t) = 0$. Denote $r_a(t) - r_l(t) = b$ and the right-hand side of equation 97 $f_b(LA(t))$. Note that $f_0'(0) = 0$ but $f_0'' \neq 0$. Also, $f_b(LA(t)) < 0$ for all $r_a(t) - r_l(t) < 0$ and this equation has two equilibrium points,

$LA(t) = \mp\sqrt{\frac{r_l(t)-r_a(t)}{r_a(t)}}$. When $r_a(t) - r_l(t) > 0$, likewise the equation has a pair of equilibria, $LA(t) = \mp\sqrt{\frac{r_a(t)-r_l(t)}{r_a(t)}}$. A saddle-node bifurcation is said to occur as the system moves through $r_a(t) - r_l(t) = 0$ (Hirsch, Smale & Devaney, 2013, p 176). The system can be regarded as an exemplification of 'loans making advances' in a modification of the Schumpeter-Keynes maxim. However, we have defined our state vector in a fashion. Interchange the numerator and the denominator and we would have advances making loans in the neoclassical manner.

We proceed to calculate the Markovian Nash Equilibrium of the game.

The central bank now operates on the assumption that the bank uses a state-dependent strategy $r_l(LA(t))$.

We have

$$H^{CB}(LA(t), r_a(t), r_l(LA(t)) = \pi^{CB}(LA(t), r_a(t), r_l(LA(t))) + \lambda(t)\{[r_a(t) - r_l(LA(t)]LA(t)\} \qquad 85'$$

Maximizing with respect to the deposit rate, 86′ is identical to 86.

$$\lambda(t)LA(t) = -D(t) \qquad 86'$$

Substituting this expression into the Hamiltonian, the maximized Hamiltonian is

$$H^{CB*} = \pi^{CB}\big(LA(t), r_a(t), r_l(LA(t)\big) - \frac{[r_a(t)-r_l(LA(t))]}{LA(t)} D(t) \qquad 87'$$

A term is added to the companion equation 88.

$$\dot{\lambda}(t) = r_a\lambda(t) - H_{LA}^{CB*} = r_a\lambda(t) - r_a + \frac{r_a - r_l}{LA^2} - \frac{r_l^{'}}{LA} \qquad 88'$$

The solution is, earlier remarks about loans and the loan rate applying,

$$\lambda(t) = -e^{\int r_a(t)dt} \int e^{\int r_a(t)}[r_a - \frac{r_a - r_l}{LA^2} + \frac{r_l^{'}}{LA}]dt \qquad 89'$$

Substituting 89′ into 86′, the optimal strategy for the central bank is given implicitly by

$$\{e^{\int r_a(t)dt} \int e^{\int r_a(t)}[r_a - \frac{r_a - r_l}{LA^2} + \frac{r_l^{'}}{LA}]dt\}LA(t) = D(t) \qquad 90'$$

In like manner, in the case of the bank the Hamiltonian is

$$H^{B}\big(LA(t), r_a(LA(t)), r_l(t)\big) = \pi^{B}\big(LA(t), r_a(LA(t)), r_l(t)\big) + \mu(t)\{[r_a(LA(t)) - r_l(t)]LA(t)\} \qquad 91'$$

The closed-loop strategy for the bank 92′ is identical to its companion 92.

$$\mu(t)LA(t) = -L(t) \qquad 92'$$

As above, the maximized Hamiltonian turns out to be

$$H^{B*} = \pi^{B}\big(LA(t), r_a(LA(t)), r_l(t)\big) - L(t)\{[r_a(LA(t)) - r_l(t)]LA(t)\} \qquad 93'$$

The adjoint equation is

$$\dot{\mu}(t) = r_l \mu(t) - r_l + L(t)\left[r_a(LA(t)) - r_l(t) + r_a^{'}(LA(t))\right] \qquad 94'$$

The solution, in this case is

$$\mu(t) = -e^{\int r_l(t)dt} \int e^{\int r_l(t)} \left[r_l(t) - L(t)[r_a(LA(t)) - r_l(t) - r_a^{'}(LA(t))]\right] dt \qquad 95'$$

Likewise, the optimal bank strategy is given implicitly by

$$\{e^{\int r_l(t)dt} \int e^{\int r_l(t)} \left[r_l(t) - L(t)[r_a(LA(t)) - r_l(t) + r_a^{'}(LA(t))]\right] dt\}LA(t) = L(t) \qquad 96'$$

Finally, the evolution of the state is determined by as above taking the ratio of 90′ to 96′ and substituting in a.

$$\dot{LA}(t) = [r_a(t) - r_l(t)]\left[\{e^{\int[(r_a(t) - r_l(t)} \int e^{\int[r_a(t) - r_l(t)]} \frac{r_a(t) - \frac{r_a(t) - r_l(t)}{LA(t)^2} + \frac{r_l^{'}(t)}{LA(t)}}{\left[r_l(t) - L(t)\left[r_a(t) - r_l(t) + r_a^{'}(t)\right]\right]} dt\}\right] \qquad 97'$$

We refer to our discussion following 97, the only difference with 97′ being indicators of elasticities of response of both players to the state of the world in the form of the two derivatives. First, we have the identical equilibrium point at the origin defined by the identity of the two interest rates. Other equilibria are defined by the roots of the following quadratic equation in the 'numerator' of the expression $LA(t)^2 + \frac{r_l^{'}(t)}{r_a(t)} LA(t) - \frac{r_a(t) - r_l(t)}{r_a(t)} = 0$. At the same time, the 'denominator' $\frac{LA(t)^2}{r_a(t)} \left[r_l - L(t)[r_a(t) - r_l(t) + r_a^{'}(t)\right]$, must not vanish at the origin. Clearly, the signs of $r_a^{'}(t)$ the responsiveness of the polity reaction function in the denominator and $r_l^{'}(t)$ the elasticity of the private sector response are critical to the solution. A common understanding of Fed policy during the Greenspan era was that Fed and financial responses caused and effected each other. That is to say, the signs of the derivatives were both positive or negative. As a countervailing force to this positive feedback, the authorities can embed an inverse supply function whose shape is the opposite of the behavioural function of the private party.

Our initial condition is a state of affairs when the economy is in a macroeconomic and growth steady state near the origin of activity. Savings in the form of deposits equals investment and banks earn a zero profit margin. As financial intermediation grows, deposits may not keep apace of demands for loans from banks by purchase executives. It is sufficient but not necessary to consider the dominating returns offered by financial markets. Central banks can step in offering advances at some price. In order, however, to keep in sync with the preferences of a putative representative depositor, both quantity and price must correspond to the dictates of utility maximization. We have taken the correspondence to be complete. Our definition of the state vector subsumes two systemic stability norms. In the case of both open-loop and closed-loop strategies, the state vector is driven by loans and advances, their quantities and their prices. In the case of closed-loop behavior when both agents respond to the current state, elasticities of response are critical. Countercyclical policy is at work. Both depositors and borrowers will respond positively or negatively to the state of the world. The response of the authorities should be counter or opposite to that of the private sector as a built-in stabilizer/inducer. Once the shape of the demand/supply function of the central bank is embedded into the system, the policy stance would be credible.

In case the movement of the two strategies in equilibrium is in opposite directions, the appellation 'strategic substitutes' can be applied to them. In experimental tests of Cournot markets when actions are strategic substitutes, the best response to an expectation of deviation from the Nash outcome is a deviation of equal magnitude but opposite sign on the other side (Davis, 2016). In contrast, in experimental tests of Bertrand models of the kind when actions are strategic complements, optimization, herding, and inertia turn out to be similar. The implication is that a variation of the institutional context can improve market outcomes. The regime would be an illustration of a feedback rule, simultaneously the solution of a one-shot optimization problem and dependent on the state vector in the period under consideration.

The standard model of interest-rate targeting, Taylor rules et al is unhelpful in illuminating and recommending policy for a world in which recession is persistent. We build a framework where the central bank is concerned with activity through the intermediation of banks. Projects which employ people and are environmentally friendly may be cherry picked. Both the quantum of central bank advances and its price matter.

7.2 Fiscal Domination

G-L matrices hark back to early eras of national income accounting which stemmed from the urgency of practical policy making. Indeed, going back as far as Petty in 1665 the discipline of double-entry booking was used to make the case for progressive taxation rather than equitable forms of taxation to support activity (Bos, 2011). Later, Lowe in 1823 used national income data to connect the tax burden and taxable income remaining after subsistence income that could not be taxed was deducted. The context in all cases was slumps and widespread poverty. Unsurprisingly, the wealthy were unhappy with the enterprise and early national income accountants were either exiled or fell out of favour. In our times, the development of national income accounts has flowered with the growth of democracy.

Developing the innovation of section 5.3 and picking up on the hint dropped in section 6.2.3, we show how the tax weapon can be used to extinguish capital gains. The question of the long-run sustainability of public debt has been addressed in a Kaleckian framework (Laski & Walther, 2013). Primary deficits can close a long-term structural saving-investment gap because public debt can always be monetized by a central bank, obviating the need to pay interest at all. Naturally, this is a luxury not afforded to countries of the Eurozone and the main impulse behind the Mosler-Pilkington scheme. Another route is lowering household savings through redistributive measures like higher wealth taxes. In another Kaleckian Departmental depiction of the Eurozone crisis, Cockshott & Zacharaiah, 2013, observe that in the aftermath lending to the working class and middle class was constrained. The household sector became a net lender. However, the working class did not become a net lender. Rentiers and workers are aggregated in the category household sector. Working class borrowing fell and savings by the propertied class increased. Accordingly, the market for Basics narrowed, aggravating the recession. In this context, even expropriatory taxation of the rentiers might not be stabilising. Taxation, in this sense, is a non-equivalent transfer of value.

We postulate that the value of long-term bonds must not decrease for reasons already adduced in section 6.2.3. Indeed, long-term bonds that are issued at low interest rates will sell at large discounts to their face values when market interest rates rise (Baker & Diagne, 2013). Secondly, it is sufficient if not necessary, to hark back to historical epochs like 1776-1920 when the American Congress specified purposes for which the proceeds of a bond sale could be used (Hall & Sargent, 2015). The illustration in this case was infrastructure like the Panama Canal. After a bond had been redeemed either through maturity or refinancing, it could not be reissued. Thirdly, the belief that if the bonds purchased lose their value because, say, a government defaults, the burden falls on taxpayers is false (Hellwig, 2015). Using newly produced fiat money to acquire assets provides a windfall to the central bank and ultimately the Treasury. The windfall is not recorded in the central bank balance sheet because the new money is listed as a liability. However, the present discounted value of the cash flows flowing from the assets is positive and the present value of the attendant debt service is nil. All losses that may subsequently be attached to the assets will detract from the windfall gain but cannot make the net return from the assets negative. We assume that only long-term bonds are availed of to finance the budget deficit. Denote G and T as the flow of fresh nominal government expenditure and taxes in the current period respectively, BL as long-term bonds and p_{bL} the price of long-term bonds.

Familiarly,

$$\Delta BL p_{bL} = G - T + BL_{-1} \qquad 98$$

We know that Haig-Simons income YD_{HS} must be added to the disposable income of households. Assuming that only households hold government bonds, $YD_{HS} = YD + \Delta p_{bL} BL$. One component of the first term on the right-hand side is the wage bill. The second term is rentier income. Also, recall that disposable income is income minus taxes paid. We also recall the famous Godley breakup

$$\Delta BL \Delta p_{bL} = \Delta BL p_{bL} + BL \Delta p_{bL} \qquad 99$$

Two possible tax scenarios emerge. The first is a tax on wages $T = \theta WB$. Substituting equation 98 into 99,

$$\Delta BL \Delta p_{bL} = G - \theta WB + BL_{-1} + BL \Delta p_{bL} \qquad 100$$

The nondecreasing value of bonds (a positive left-hand side) can be ensured by minimising the negative items on the right-hand side. The only discretionary element is the tax rate. Thus, $\theta = 0$ will suffice. However, we cannot exclude the possibility of dramatic capital losses. Indeed, if the fall in the price level is in the nature of the bursting of a bubble the negative value of the term on the extreme right might exceed the sum of the two positive terms. The value of government bonds crashes.

The other case is one where capital gains is taxed $T = \theta \Delta p_{bL} BL$. This time equation 98 becomes

$$\Delta BL \Delta p_{bL} = G + BL_{-1} + \Delta p_{bL} BL(1 - \theta) \qquad 101$$

Capital gains/losses will evaporate with $\theta = 1$. Furthermore, the increase in the value of government bonds will be more or less coterminous with government expenditure. A famous Kalecki aphorism applied to the capitalist class can be twisted. Under the circumstances, governments earn in a sense what they spend. Government expenditure on schools and hospitals benefits all classes. Furthermore, only capital gains are confiscated. In the case of a capital loss, the tax is a rebate. Along with the coupon, thereby, the instrument provides a preferred habitat for a class of investors.

We note that none of the above is required to extinguish capital gains. G&L work out a formulation of Keynes's famous squares law that connects the square of the current rate of return on long-term bonds with the rate that is required to wipe out capital gains. We provide an equivalent derivation. They deduce the following definition of the pure rate of return on bonds where the long-term rate of interest r_{bL} is the reciprocal of the bond price p_{bL}.

$$r_{bL} = (1 + p_{bL} - p_{bL-1}) / p_{bL-1} \qquad 102$$

Since $r_{bL} = 1 / p_{bL}$, equation 102 delivers the following difference equation:

$$r^2_{bL} = r_{bL} . r_{bL-1} + r_{bL-1} - 1 \qquad 103$$

In the steady state, the rate of return must be unity thereby eliminating capital gains. The solution of this nonlinear difference equation is another matter and the complexity reflects the difficulty in solving out for the long-term rate of interest. Relatedly, Dean Baker, 2016, has operationalised a "financial transactions tax" (FTT). The quantum would be borne entirely by the financial industry and not private holders of stock and pension funds. According to his computations, trading volume is elastic with reference to price. Any drop in trading volume flowing from the imposition of the tax would reduce costs for end users by a far greater amount than the tax would increase them. The corollaries are that the FTT would dent inequality since finance is the main source of income for the highest earners and the volatility brought about by continuous trading would be punctured. Short termism would be curbed and the lengthening of the working period restored.

Absent the unit payout per period, the riskless bond partakes of the nature of "sovereign currency" in the articulation of Wray and Liu, 2014, and prompts an older interpretation of the backing of government money. The model would have to be extended to the holding of bills and the activity of commercial banks. The government could be the "employer of last resort", the wage bill entailed by the projects on one side supported by the issue of money on the other. Assuming, as usual, a high propensity to consume by the working class, their incomes return to firms who redeem their debts to the banks.

7.3 International Relations: Competition and Conflict

We use the G&L to work out the logical connections between two countries. In a two-country model, 'home' is denoted by £ and 'foreign' by \$. A subscript will distinguish central banks from others. Variables reflect current values and a -1 subscript will signify the value of the variable in the previous period. Thus, $B^{\$}_{cb£-1}$ would denote bonds issued by the 'foreign' central bank (the superscript) in the previous period and held by the domestic central bank (the subscript).xr is the exchange rate, the superscript identifying the currency. An overall view from which submatrices will be drawn is as follows.

		Production firms			
	Households			Government	Central Bank
		Current	Capital		
Consumption	$-C^{£}$	$+C^{£}$			
Investment		$+I^{£}$	$-I^{£}$		
Government Expenditures	$+G^{£}$			$-G^{£}$	
Wages	$+WB^{£}$	$-WB^{£}$			
Taxes	$-T^{£}$			$+T^{£}$	
Interest payments	$+r^{£}.B^{£}_{£}$ $+r^{\$}.B^{\$}_{£}.xr^{\$}$				$+r^{£}.B^{£}_{cb£}$ $+r^{\$}.B^{\$}_{cb£}.xr^{\$}$
Change in loans		$+\Delta L^{£}$	$-\Delta L^{£}$		
Change in money	$-\Delta H^{£}$				$+\Delta H^{£}$
Change in bills	$-\Delta B^{£}_{£}$			$+\Delta B^{£}$	$-\Delta B^{£}_{cb£}$
	$-\Delta B^{\$}_{£}.xr^{\$}$				$-\Delta B^{\$}_{cb£}.xr^{\$}$

Usually, assets are held by all classes. Households as well as firms borrow from banks, banks issue equity. The box above is not as dense as it might be. In order to focus on our thesis, we save on coefficients without any loss of generality. The difference equation systems decomposed from this matrix will be non-homogenous. The diagonal matrices of coefficients will highlight the autarkic policy variables of independent central banks. The non-homogenous part will contain variables like the exchange rate which are interdependent terms.

Reversing the sequence of section of 5.3, our first scenario is one in which both governments finance their budget deficits by issuing short-term paper. In the first case, the bill issue will be only be absorbed by households in each country. We assume that only rentier income is taxed. The "euthanasia of the rentier(s)" is shown to be stable.

The equation of the fresh issue of domestic bills to support the deficit at home is

$$G^{£} - T^{£} = \Delta B^{£} - r^{£}.B^{£}_{£-1} - r^{£}.B^{£}_{\$-1}.xr^{£} \qquad 104$$

An identical equation can be written up for the 'foreign' country, the £ and the \$ symbols changing places. Each government only taxes the asset income of its residents ignoring capital gains. Thus, in the case of the home country with θ as the tax rate, we have $T^{£} = \theta^{£}.(r^{£}.B^{£}_{£-1} + r^{\$}.B^{\$}_{£-1}.xr^{\$})$. An identical tax regime holds abroad with a change of subscripts and superscripts. Transcribing the two-country model in state-space form we have

$$\begin{bmatrix} \Delta B^{£} \\ \Delta B^{\$} \end{bmatrix} = \begin{bmatrix} (1-\theta^{£})r^{£} & 0 \\ 0 & (1-\theta^{\$})r^{\$} \end{bmatrix} \begin{bmatrix} B^{£}_{£-1} \\ B^{\$}_{\$-1} \end{bmatrix} + \begin{bmatrix} G^{£} + r^{£}.B^{£}_{\$-1}.xr^{£} \\ G^{\$} + r^{\$}.B^{\$}_{£-1}.xr^{\$} \end{bmatrix} \qquad 105$$

Denoting the determinant of the matrix by D and the trace of the matrix by T, the phase portrait is stable. It is a node if $0 < D < T^2/4$ and a spiral if $0 < T^2/4 < D$. In either instance, both countries will need to set their tax rates and rates of return on their bill offerings together. While arbitrage conditions might push the latter, the former demands deep cooperation between the two countries. The nonhomogenous portion of the system suggests that all essential macroeconomic ingredients are in sync across the cycle. In the trough of activity, along with a 'low' bills interest rate and 'low' exchange rates the market in government paper will be muted. The modern trend is to underscore the quality of government expenditure. The G in the equations must be associated with handpicking of programs intimately linked with job creation (Picek, 2015). A National Public Bank can be a purchaser of last resort in the primary market.

We need perfect monetary-fiscal coordination in the next scenario. The change in the requirements when, at the other extreme, one hand of the government accepts what the other hand is offering, is due entirely to a change of sign. Its importance has already been introduced in section 5.3.1. Central bank profits from holding government bonds from either country is ploughed back into own Treasuries. Reproducing equation 104 with a change of sign and subscript we have

$$G^{£} - T^{£} = \Delta B^{£} + r^{£}.B^{£}_{cb£-1} + r^{£}.B^{£}_{cb\$-1}.xr^{£} \qquad 106$$

The counterpart of equation 105 in this case is

$$\begin{bmatrix}\Delta B^{£}\\ \Delta B^{\$}\end{bmatrix} = \begin{bmatrix}-r^{£} & 0\\ 0 & -r^{\$}\end{bmatrix}\begin{bmatrix}B^{£}_{cb£-1}\\ B^{\$}_{cb\$-1}\end{bmatrix} + \begin{bmatrix}G^{£} + r^{£}.B^{£}_{cb\$-1}.xr^{£} - T^{£}\\ G^{\$} + r^{\$}.B^{\$}_{cb£-1}.xr^{\$} - T^{\$}\end{bmatrix} \qquad 107$$

The requirements for stability are met by definition without any constraints needing to be imposed. The tax weapon has been relegated to the nonhomogenous portion of the system. In the steady-state, a ratchet equilibrium is suggested. A government deficit in a recession is accompanied by equilibrium dynamics that presuppose payments in the upswing that generate a deficit in the upswing and so on.

While output and employment are absent from the identities above, they are the 'duals' of the equations. Double-entry-bookkeeping practice is adhered to and other macroeconomic variables play their role in the background. However, if any state variable is operating at a suboptimal level it needs to be brought to the fore and the government intervention required to push or pull the economy towards the desired end must be specified. We now assume that the government deficit is supported by high-powered money or the money base *H*. That is to say $G^{£} - T^{£} = \Delta H^{£}$. Assuming away other holders of central bank money only for the sake of simplicity, central bank money is connected with private bank money *M* by the cash reserve ratio ρ. In this case, $H^{£} = \rho^{£}M^{£}$. Reverting to Macro 101, we have for the closed economy $S - I = G - T$, and savings *S* in turn equals the residual from disposable income *YD* after taxes and consumption *C*. In G&C&L, even if investment is not forthcoming inventory accumulation must be accounted for. In that case, it would be easier to ground the assumption that lines of credit with banks must be existent. Assuming away the issue of equity, investment plans call for a flow of loans L for this purpose. Therefore $I = \Delta L$. Disposable income equals the sum of the wage bill WB the interest earned on time deposits $r_m.M_{-1}$ where r_m is the deposit rate minus loans due to banks L_{-1} at a price r_l. For the moment, we assume that citizens only hold deposits in their own currencies and firms do not borrow from foreign banks. In closed-economy terms, we have

$$S^£ - I^£ = G^£ - T^£$$

$$\therefore YD^£ - C^£ - I^£ = \Delta H^£$$

$$\therefore WB^£ - C^£ + (r_m^£/\rho^£).H_{-1}^£ - r_l^£.L_{-1}^£ = \Delta H^£ + \Delta L^£$$

For notational convenience, we combine the two state variables above into one for the homogenous part of the next depiction. Define $H + L$ as A. There is a substantive justification for the choice of the first letter of the alphabet in the notation which will be explained below. With the parallel exercise carried out for the other economy, the state space representation is as follows.

$$\begin{bmatrix} \Delta A^£ \\ \Delta A^\$ \end{bmatrix} = \begin{bmatrix} r_m^£/\rho^£ - r_l^£ & 0 \\ 0 & r_m^\$/\rho^£ - r_l^\$ \end{bmatrix} \begin{bmatrix} A_{-1}^£ \\ A_{-1}^\$ \end{bmatrix} + \begin{bmatrix} WB^£ - C^£ - (r_m^£/\rho^£).H_{-1}^£ - r_l^£.L_{-1}^£ \\ WB^\$ - C^\$ - (r_m^\$/\rho^\$).H_{-1}^\$ - r_l^\$.L_{-1}^\$ \end{bmatrix}$$

Once more, across all stability criteria the suggestion is that the exchange rates be "low" enough. In a general scenario when households at home hold cash both at home and abroad and banks lend to both domestic and foreign firms the economics remains as simple. Our earlier variables would be extended to $\Delta L^£ = \Delta L_£^£ + \Delta L_\$^£.xr^£$ and $\Delta H^£ = \Delta H_£^£ + \Delta H_\$^£, xr^£$. To the disposable income of the household at home would be added the interest income earned on the foreign account $(r_m^\$/\rho^\$).H_{£-1}^\$.xr^\$$ and the firm at home might owe its foreign commercial bank creditor $r_l^\$.L_{\$-1}^\$.xr^\$$. This time the exchange rate would be added to both the requirements for stability as well as be part of the solution of the system. The loan rate at home must exceed the cash reserves ratio at home. In recent times the risk-reducing role exercised by the weapon of the cash reserves ratio in the hands of central banks has been taken over by international formulae like capital-adequacy norms of the Basel agreements (Ugolini, 2011). The central bank of the country needs to restore the power of fractional reserve banking in directing credit to particular borrowers. Eligibility Criteria for the procurement of credit must be modernised. In other words, the central bank would lend to customers mainly on the security of government bonds. Differently put, the monetary and fiscal authorities must coordinate. Recovery from the recession from 1933 to 1936 in the USA was accomplished not just through monetary policy but by bank lending to the government in order to finance the New Deal programmes. It is not that lending to the private sector increased (Koo, 2011). Fiscal policy was paramount in keeping output and the money supply from contracting. From the equation, the loan rate exceeding the deposit rate might be part of the necessary conditions for stability. The wedge might also be sufficient (Vredin, 2015). We draw attention, though, to the cash reserve ratio which can range over the unit interval in the interest of stability. The existence and stability of a dynamical real-monetary system depend upon the coordination of private money and central bank money. Private bank money and central bank money can peacefully coexist on the authority of historians. For instance, the period 1914-1955 was unique in American history because it was the only time national bank notes and Federal Reserve notes circulated at the same time (Weber, 2015). The takeaway for today is that the grant of the monopoly of note issue power is not completely persuasive. Since the substantive content of private money and State money is different, they will have a different form. Why then the Federal Reserve Notes? The reason, appropriate to modern times, is that national bank notes failed to provide an elastic currency. The private banking system did not evolve a mechanism by means of which banks could expand their resources during times of stress. The history of the Bank of England has provided at least four pearls of wisdom (Williamson, 2015): (i) The link between a central bank and the fiscal authority is inextricable; (ii) The power of the central bank resides in its monopoly of liability issue; (iii) Central bank intermediation is of an order of involvement not too far removed from commercial bank intermediation; (iv) It is unnecessary to be handed an explicit central banker objective function. In our framework, the exigencies of the dynamics dictate the policy reactions. In the present, countries across the globe are reinventing nationalization of banks in the interest of directing credit and creating employment. The possible trinity is posited in heterodox accounts that combine capital controls so as to deliver a stable exchange rate and assist in limiting destabilising leverage in domestic balance sheets (Epstein, 2015). Presiding over the trio would be a so-called Development Central Bank concerned as much with employment and output as with inflation.

The first two regimes of this section depicted in equations 105 and 107 have been called the "pure auto-economy" by the great John Hicks (G&L, 2007, pp 55-56). The last economy is a development of what he termed an "overdraft economy". In such an economy, the central bank would pump reserves A into private banks at a price r_a for meeting their statutory requirements. In a further elaboration, fresh government expenditures are financed by loans ΔL_g taken from private banks. We assume that advances from central banks to private banks are scrupulously for the purpose of supporting approved loans. Indeed, discount window operations in a line of thinking originating with Minsky should be incisive and fleshed out particularly if the central bank is to climb to the 'commanding heights of the economy' (Argitis, 2015; Wray 2015). As in the first section of this chapter, the operation is intended to be a window to banks, their balance sheets, income records and competence of their clients. There is nothing in law and economics that eschews banks being thereby "in the Bank". Borrowing from the central bank is short term and against approved classes of securities. The short-term nature of the banks' debt to the central bank and the short-term nature of the business debt that is eligible for collateral create a steady dynamic of origination and cancellation between private debt, bank deposits, and borrowing. When the central bank changes the terms on which it accommodates bank borrowing, the contracts between banks and business and households are automatically affected. In discount window operations, the quantity of reserves are determined by the forces of demand and supply. The central bank it is that decides the discount rate.

We have been silent on inflation right through and deal with the matter now. Defining the domestic unit cost of production as $UC^{£} = WB^{£}/y^{£}$ where $y^{£}$ is real output at home, the rate of cost inflation π_C is defined as the rate of change in unit costs. In that case, $UC^{£} = (1 + \pi_C)UC_{-1}$. The set of factors, monetary and nonmonetary, in the extreme right-hand vector in the equation above with negative signs attached to them would be an antidote to the rate of change of the wage bill. Inflation is not a monetary phenomenon alone. Indeed, base money, both domestic and foreign, would be counterpoises to domestic cost-plus forces. Along with the components of the bank spread, increased bank borrowing and lending both at home and abroad would serve to mitigate the impact of inflation on the stability of both. These radically non mainstream observations are the outcome of not throwing in a quantity theory equation into our model. The definition of aggregate profits constituting with aggregate wages the other component of another familiar breakup of National Income will suffice to trace the simple dynamics. A surge of borrowing at home or abroad today is a positive item in the capital account of firms if a negative item in the current account. Profits are increased on capital account while the interest payments due on borrowings 'last year' will be a negative item. Lively financial intermediation implies dynamic deposit (base money) activity in this credit-driven scenario. Savings in banks are made out of wage income. All these flows lower the wage bill at a given level of income.

All that is left to connect with elements of current discussion elsewhere are financial codes and speed-breakers. The question, to recap, is whether the task should be left to the central bank or an Independent Office or a different Office either at home or in Basel. Our model can easily be extended to include these elements. We need only to include equity emissions by banks and firms and capital adequacy norms arise naturally as in earlier chapters. They would be elements in the coefficient matrices of appropriately-specified dynamical systems.

Chapter 8

Conclusions

Macro is an order of explanation different from micro. The unwary scholar is likely to fall into the pitfalls of the fallacies of composition and division in moving from the former to the latter and the latter to the former if not careful. General equilibrium macroeconomists following Robert Lucas hold that the division in pedagogy is illusory by being ignorant of the capital theory debates that the best minds in the profession wrestled with in the last century and introducing money into their models through abstract, that is empirically and institutionally empty, devices. In contrast, money qua the government bond rises from the past and the present in different places in our accounts. The banking system is shown to be hierarchically ordered with the central bank and commercial banks at different ends of the same spectrum. Consequently, a Plan to employ a large number of people on meaningful and environmentally-friendly projects can be effected by either. The founding fathers of the Chicago School would have disassociated themselves from the nonmonetary neoclassical economics of the new classical vintage. Indeed, many of the creative policy responses we have proposed have their origin paraphrasing Keynes in the "right ... ideas of (these) economists and political philosophers". At the same time, we acknowledge some imaginative work in the DSGE genre that has introduced flesh-and-blood banks and systems that are crisis-prone. The work still remains wedded to the micro foundations of macroeconomics research strategy. Agents are not assumed to operate under system-wide constraints not of their making. They are forward looking, history does not obtrude. The labour market in terms of both price and quantity does not command special attention. Neither does the division of the economy into Departments or into town and country. The latter breakup is indispensable for modeling the transition of economies from pre-capitalist to the capitalist mode of production. Finance can supervene in a productive or a rapacious manner. At root the economy is regarded as an entity described by commodities and technology with a monetary-financial superstructure that is prone to topple over and sometimes damage the base. A general equilibrium with market-clearing still remains the cornerstone. In contrast, SFC macroeconomics along with other companion schools of thought view the economy as a multi-layered and indistinguishable money-financial-real system. "Equilibrium" as only Joan Robinson could put it "is blither". The economy is always aflutter and at this time of writing and for many quarters to come not escape from the maw of a black hole which sucks in more and more of the unemployed who, after a few years, join their compatriots in the nether world of the statistics-free. Positive flows in hires in the last quarter is no compensation for the vast stock of humanity that has vanished. The macroeconomic organs of the State, monetary and fiscal, must constantly be combat-ready to encounter fluctuations big and small. Weapons like interest rates are never sharp and tend to rust quickly. Following Abba Lerner, fiat money must support government employment-generating schemes following the exigencies of the numbers of the times. Anything else would be committing the fallacy of division, holding that government money is the same as private money, government expenditure is the same as private expenditure. People cannot print money for general acceptance and their expenditure must match their income in the long run. In addition, new instruments must be forged and we have the wisdom of the ancients tucked away in workshops and maps to guide the way. The "laws of motion of capitalism" are captured in different ways in the tales told above. The open-loop and closed-loop feedback loops indicate that battlegrounds cannot be drawn on chicken-and-egg questions. Causal arrows swerve and savings and investment are equally important, as are deposits and loans. Interest rates are neither desirably 'low' or 'high' per se. At the same time, the predilections of the classes driving them and being driven by them are no less important. In particular, their degrees of (im)patience matter in the models. All must go long in the joint interest of the accumulation of capital. However, the pull of finance will not be resisted and capitalists and workers will choose to short the system. The arbitrage principle will continue to exert its magical spell. The State must be another player in the game instituting policies and menus of options that private agents find not inferior to market offerings. Thereby, they can steer economies towards long-run green growth without violating the Pareto principle.

References

Amato, M., L. Fantacci, D.B. Papadimitriou and G. Zezza, 2016, Going forward from B to A? Proposals for the Eurozone Crisis, Jerome Levy Economics Institute of Bard College Working Paper No 866

Argitis, G., 2015, Alternative Monetary Policy and Central Banking, FESSUD (Financialisation, Economy, Society and Sustainable Development) Working Paper No 82

Assa, J., 2016, The Financialization of GDP and its Implications for Macroeconomic Debates, The New School for Social Research, Department of Economics Working Paper 10/2016

Balmann, A. and V. Valentinov, 2016, Structural Change in Agri-Food Chains: new relations between farm sector, food industry and retail sector, paper presented at 149th EAE seminar Rennes, France, October 27-28, 2016

Baker, D. and S. Diagne, 2013, Financial Engineering: The Simple Way to Reduce Government Debt Burdens, Center for Economic and Policy Research, Issue Brief

Baker, D., 2016, Reining in Wall Street to Benefit All Americans, CEPR Report: Discovering Government

Banaji, J., 2016, Merchant Capitalism, Peasant Households, and Industrial Capitalism, *Journal of Agrarian Change*, 16, 3, 410-431

Bayoumi, T., 2015, The Dog That Didn't Bark: The Strange Case of Domestic Policy Cooperation in the "New Normal", IMF Working Paper 15/156

Becker, S.O., S. Pfaff and J. Rubin, 2016, Causes and Consequences of the Protestant Reformation, Warwick Economics Research Paper Series No 1005

Bibow, J., 2015, The Euro's Saviour? Assessing the ECB's Crisis Management Performance and Potential for Crisis, Levy Economics Institute of Bard College Working Paper No 845

Blancheton, B., 2015, Towards a tacit low-degree independent central banking model?, Cahiers de Group de Recherche en Economie Théorique et Appliquée (GRETLA) n^0 2015-17

Bos, F., 2011, Three centuries of macro-economic statistics, MPRA Paper No. 35391, Eagle Economic & Statistics Working Paper 2011-02

Braun, B., 2015, Governing the future: the European Central Bank's expectation management during the Great Moderation, *Economy and Society*, 44, 3, 367-391

Bresser-Pereira, L.C., 2015, Reflecting on new developmentalism and classical developmentalism, Sao Paulo School of Economics Working Paper 395

__________________, 2016, Democracy and growth in pre-industrial countries, FGV Sao Paulo School of Economics Working Paper 410

Bridges, J.,C. Jackson and D. McGregor, 2017, Down in the slumps: the role of credit in five decades of recessions, Bank of England Staff Working Paper No 659

Brisset, N., 2016, Institutions as defining Emergent Phenomena: Redefining Downward Causation, GREDEG Working Paper 2016-30

Byres, T.J., 2016, In Pursuit of Capitalist Agrarian Transition, *Journal of Agrarian Change*, 16, 3, 432-451

Cauwels, P. and D. Sornette, 2012, The Illusion of the Perpetual Money Machine, Swiss Finance Institute Research Paper No 12-40

Cockshott, P. and D. Zacharaiah, 2016, Conservation Laws, financial entropy and the Eurozone crisis, Economics Discussion Paper No 2013-36

Corsetti, G., L. Dedola, M. Jarociński, B. Maćkowiak and S. Schmidt, 2016, Macroeconomic Stabilization, Monetary-Fiscal Interactions, and Europe's Monetary Union, Cambridge-INET Working Paper Series No 2016/27

Dadush, U., 2016, Industrial Policy: A Guide for the Perplexed, OCP Policy Center Policy Brief 16/05

Dantas, F. and L. Randall Wray, 2017, Falling Labour Force Participation: Demographics or Lack of Jobs, Levy Economics Institute of Bard College One-Pager No 53

Davanzati, G.F., 2015, Nicholas Kaldor on Endogenous Money and Increasing Returns, Post Keynesian Economics Study Group Working Paper 1505

Davis, D., 2016, Experimental Methods for the General Economist: Five Lessons from the Lab, Presidential Address, 85th Annual Meeting of the Southern Economics Association, New Orleans, Louisiana

Davis, J. B., 2016, The Continuing Relevance of Keynes's Philosophical Thinking: Reflexivity, Complexity, and Uncertainty, GREDEG Working Paper No 2016-38

Dechaux, P., 2014, Proving the existence of macropsychological phenomena? The Katona-Tobin controversy over the predictive value of attitudinal data, Documents de travail du Centre d'Economie de la Sorbonne 2015.11

__________, 2015, Conceptualising the formation and role of expectations before 1950: George Katona's thought, Documents de travail du Centre d'Economie de la Sorbonne 2015.10

de Grauwe, P., 2015, Greece is solvent but not illiquid: What should the ECB do?, CEPS Commentary

Degryse H., T. Lambers and A. Schwienbacher, 2013, The Political Economy of Financial Systems: Evidence from Suffrage Reforms in the last two centuries, European Banking Center Discussion Paper No 2013-008; also CentER Discussion Paper No 2013-046, Tilburg University

Esen O. and A.O. Binati, 2013, The Minsky Perspective on Macroprudential Policies, University of Massachusetts Amherst, Political Economy Research Institute Working Paper No.308

Dockner, E., S. Jørgensen, N. Van Long and G. Sorger, 2000, *Differential Games in economics and management science*, Cambridge, Cambridge University Press

Domanski, D., R. Moessner and W.R. Nelson, 2014, Central Banks as Lenders of Last Resort: experiences during the 2007-2010 crisis and lessons for the future, Division of Research & Statistics and Monetary Affairs, Finance and Economics Discussion Paper 2014-10, Federal Reserve Board, Washington DC

Dosi, G., L. Marengo and A. Novolari, 2016, Institutions are neither Autistic Maximizers nor Flocks of Birds: Self-Organization, Power, and Learning in

Human Organizations, LEM Institute of Economics, Scuola Superiore Sant'Anna Working Paper 2016/38

Dreschler, D., J. Jülting and T. Xenogiani, 2008, Is Informal Normal? Towards More and Better Jobs, Poverty in Focus, International Poverty Centre No 16, pp 8-9

Epstein, G., 2015, Development Central Banking: A review of issues and experiences, ILO Employment Policy Department EMPLOYMENT Working Paper No 182

Fine, B., K. Bayliss and M. Robertson, 2016, Housing and Water in light of Financialization and "Financialization", FESSUD Working Paper No 156

Fisher, R.W., 2013, Ending "Too Big to Fail": A Proposal for Reform Before It's Too Late (with Reference to Patrick Henry, Complexity and Reality), Remarks before the Committee for the Republic, Washington DC

Flandreau, M. and S. Ugolini, 2014, The crisis of 1866, Graduate Institute of International and Development Studies, Geneva, Working Paper 10/2014

Foley, D. K. and T. R. Michl, 1999, *Growth and Distribution*, Cambridge, Massachusetts, Harvard University Press

Fontana, G. and R. Realfonzo, 2017, Introduction: Augusto Graziani and recent advances in the monetary theory of production, *Metroeconomica*, 68, 2, 202-204

Ford Foundation/Levy Economics Institute of Bard College, 2012, Improving governance of the Government safety net in financial crisis

Franck, R. & O. Galor, 2015, Is Industrialization Conducive to Long-Run Prosperity? CESifo Working Paper No 5354

Frey, C.B., 2015, How the digital economy could lead to secular stagnation, *Scientific American*, 312, 1

Frigero, P., 2017, Reconsidering communication regarding economic phenomena: some hints from a complexity approach, Università Degli Studi Di Torino, Department of Economics and Statistics Working Paper No 40

Godley, W. and F. Cripps, 1983, *Macroeconomics*, Oxford, Oxford University Press

Godley, W. and M. Lavoie, 2007, *Monetary Economics*, basingstoke, Hampshire, palgrave macmillan

Goodhart, C.A.E. and J.A. Meinhard, 2015, A Commentary on Patrizio Lainà's 'Proposals for Full-Reserve Banking: A Historical Survey from David Ricardo to Martin Wolf', *Economic Thought*, 4, 2, 20-31

Goodhart, C.A.E., 2017, Whither Central Banking? LSE Research Online, http//prints.lse.ac.uk/69279

Gorton, G.B., 2013, The Federal Reserve and Financial Regulation: The First Hundred Years, NBER Working Paper 19292

Gorton, G.B. and G. Ordoñez, 2014, How Central Banks End Crises, PIER Working Paper No 14-205

Green, R., 1992, *Classical Theories of Money, Output and Inflation*, London, St. Martin's Press

Greenwood-Nimmo, M. and A. Tarassow, 2013, A Macroeconometric Assessment of Minky's Financial Instability Hypothesis, Universität Hamburg, Department of Socioeconomics Discussion Paper 6/2013

Greider, W., 2013, "Unusual and Exigent": How the Fed can Jumpstart the Real Economy, Levy Economics Institute of Bard College Policy Note 2013/8

Grubb, F., 2013, The Continental Dollar: How the American Revolution was Financed with Paper Money, University of Delaware, Alfred Lerner College of Business and Economics Department of Economics Working Paper No 2013-10

_______, 2016, Colonial Virginia's paper money regime 1755-1774: Value decomposition and performance, NBER Working Paper 21881.

Grieve, R. H., 2015, Revisiting Cantillon's Admirable Theory of Distribution and Value, Strathclyde Discussion Paper in Economics 15-06

Hall, G.J., and T.J. Sargent, 2015, A History of US debt limits, NBER Working Paper 21799

Hanappi, H. and M. Scholz-Waeckerle, 2016, Evolutionary Political Economy: Content and Methods, MPRA Paper No 75447

Heise, A., 2016, Whither economic complexity? A new heterodox economic paradigm or just another variation within the mainstream? Discussion Papers, Zentrum für Ökonomische und Soziologische Studien No 58

Hellwig, M., 2015, Financial Stability and Monetary Policy, Reprints of the Max Planck Institute for Research on Collective Goods, Bonn, 2015/10

Hillinger, C., 2010, The Crisis and Beyond: Thinking Outside the Box, Economics The Open-Access, Open-Assessment E-Journal, Discussion Paper 2010-2

Hirsch, M.W., S. Smale and R.L. Devaney, 2013, *Differential Equations, Dynamical Systems, and an Introduction to Chaos*, Oxford, Academic Press

Ho, T-J., 2016, The Social Provisioning Process and Heterodox Economics, MPRA Paper No 72384

Humpage, O.F., 2014, Independence within – not of – Government: The Emergence of the Federal Reserve as a Modern Central Bank, Federal Reserve Bank of Cleveland Working Paper 14-02

Humphries, J. and J. Weisdorf, 2016, Unreal Wages? A New Empirical Foundation for the Study of Living Standards and Economic Growth in England, 1260-1860, University of Oxford Discussion Papers in Economic and Social History No 147

Irwin, G., 2008, Is the World Returning to 1970s stagflation? School of Oriental and African Studies, Centre for Development Policy and Research Development Viewpoint No 15

Jackson, T., V. Peter and A.N. Ali, 2016, Towards a Stock-Flow Consistent Ecological Macroeconomics, WWWFOREUROPE Working Paper No 114

Jonasson, E., 2008, Rural Non-Farm Jobs-A Pathway out of Poverty? Poverty in Focus, International Poverty Centre No 16, pp 24-25

Kalecki, M., 1943, *Studies in Economic Dynamics*, London, Allen and Unwin

__________, 1953, *Theory of Economic Dynamics*, London, Allen and Unwin

__________,1971, *Selected Essays on the Dynamics of the Capitalist Economy: 1933-1970*, Cambridge, Cambridge University Press

___________,1976, *Essays on Developing Economies*, Sussex, The Harvester Press

Karayalcin, C., 2015, Property Rights and the Great Divergence: Europe 1500-1800, *International Review of Economics and Finance*

Koo, R.C., 2011, The world is in balance sheet recession: causes, cures, problems, *real-world economics review*, 58, 19-37.

Kopsidis, M. and M. Ivanov, 2015, Was Gerschenkron right? Bulgarian agricultural growth during the Interwar period in light of modern development economics, European Historical Economic Society Working Paper No 82

Krainer, R.E., 2010, Towards a Program for Financial Stability, Università degli Studi di Urbino "Carlo Bo" Facultà di Economia Working Paper-EMS #2010/08

Kregel, J., 2010, Is This the Minsky Moment for Reform of Financial Regulation, Levy Economics Institute of Bard College Working Paper No 586

_______, 2014, Minsky and Dynamic Prudential Regulation, Levy Economics Institute of Bard College Public Policy Brief No 131

Lainà P., 2015, Proposals for Full-Reserve Banking: A Historical Survey from David Ricardo to Martin Wolf, *Economic Thought*, 4, 2, 1-19

Laski, K., and H. Walther, 2013, Kalecki's Profit Equation after 60 Years, The Vienna Institute for International Economic Studies Working Paper 100

Leeper, E.M. and J.M. Nason, 2014, Bringing Financial Stability into Monetary Policy, Center for Applied Economics and Policy Research (CAEPR) Working Paper # 2014-03

Lenton, P., M. Masiye and P. Mosley, 2017, Taxpayer's dilemma: how can 'fiscal contracts' work in developing countries? The University of Sheffield Economics Research Paper Series No 2017004

Long, N.V., 2010, *Survey of Dynamic Games in Economics*, Singapore, World Scientific

Mazzucato, M. and G. Semieniuk, 2017, Public Financing of Innovation: new questions, *Oxford Review of Economic Policy*, 33, 1, 24-48

Medio A. and M. Lines, 2001, *Nonlinear dynamics: a primer*, Cambridge, Cambridge University Press

McCallum, B.T., 2012, The role of money in New Keynesian Models, Central Reserve Bank of Peru, Working Paper DT No 2012-019

McKinley, T., 2008, The Globalisation of Inflation and Misguided Monetary Policy, School of Oriental and African Studies, Centre for Development Policy and Research, Development Viewpoint No.14

McKinnon, R.M., 2014, Hot Money Flows, Cycles in Primary Commodity Prices and Financial Control in Developing Countries, Fondation Pour Les Études et Recherches Sur Le Développment International Working Paper 109

Milanovic, B., 2013, The return of "patrimonial capitalism": review of Thomas Piketty's Capital in the 21st century, MPRA Paper No. 52384

Minsky, H., 1986, *Stabilizing an Unstable Economy*, New Haven, Yale University Press

Mongin, P., 2017, A Game-Theoretic Analysis of the Waterloo Campaign and some comments on the Analytic Narrative project, MPRA Paper No 78029

Nersiyan, Y., 2015, The Repeal of the Glass-Steagall Act and Consequences for Crisis Response, Ford Foundation/Levy Economics Institute of Bard College, Reforming the Fed's Policy Response in the Era of Shadow Banking, Chapter 4

Papadimitriou, D.B., M. Nikiforos and G. Zezza, 2015, Greece: Conditions and Strategies for Economic Recovery, Jerome Levy Economics Institute of Bard College, Strategic Analysis

_______________, 2016, A Complementary Currency and Direct Job Creation Hold the Key to Greek Recovery, Jerome Levy Economics Institute of Bard College One-Pager No 52

Palley, T.I., 2017, Monetary Policy and the Punch Bowl: The case for quantitative policy and wage growth targeting, Macroeconomic Policy Institute Working Paper No 177

Passarella, M.V., 2016, A Marx 'Crisis' Model: The Reproduction Schemes Revisited, Post Keynesian Economics Study Group Working Paper 1610

Pérez-Caldentey, E. and M. Vernengo, 2012, The Euro Imbalances and Financial Deregulation: A Post-Keynesian Interpretation of the European Debt Crisis, Levy Economics Institute Working Paper No 702

Picek, O., 2015, A national public bank to finance a euro zone government: Getting the funds for investment and recovery packages, New School for Social Research, Department of Economics Working Paper 12/2015

Pilkington, P., 2013, The Continued Relevance of Tax-Backed Bonds in a Post-OMT Eurozone, Levy Economics Institute of Bard College Policy Note 2013/10

Pivetti, M., 1991, *An Essay on Money and Distribution*, London, Macmillan

Poznar, Z., 2014, Shadow Banking: The Money View, Office of Financial Research Working Paper 14-04

Quesnay, François, 1759, *Tableau Économique*

Rockoff, H., 2010, Parallel Journeys: Adam Smith and Milton Friedman on the regulation of banking, unpublished

Russi, L. and T. Ferrando, 2015, 'Capitalism A Nuh' Wi Frien': The Formatting of Farming into an Asset, from Financial Speculation to International Aid, Institute for the Study of Political Economy and Law, Research Paper Repository, International University, College of Turin

Ryan-Collins, J., T. Greenham, R. Werner and A. Jackson, 2016, *Where does money come from?* London, creative commons

Sakai, Y., 2016, Frank H. Knight on Market Thinking: Reflections on the Logic and Ethics of the Capitalist Economy, Shiga University, Center for Risk Research Discussion Paper No A-22

Scarano, G., 2013, Quantity Theory, Say's Law and Effective Demand in Money Theories, Dipartimento di Economia Università degli studi Roma Tre Working Paper n^0 181

Schumpeter, J.A., 1951, *The Theory of Economic Development*, Cambridge, Harvard University Press

Shiller, R., 2011, Irving Fisher, Debt Deflation and Crisis, Cowles Foundation Discussion Paper No 1017

Solomon S., and N. Golo, 2014, Minsky financial instability, interscale feedback, percolation and Marshall-Walras disequilibrium, unpublished

Subrun, J. and P. Turner, 2015, Bond markets and monetary policy dilemmas for the emerging markets, BIS Working Paper No. 508

Sugden, R., 2016, Ontology, Methodological Individualism, and the Foundations of the Social Sciences, *Journal of Economic Literature*, 54, 4, 1377-1389

Tesfatsion, L., 2017, Modeling Economic Systems as Locally-Constructive Sequential Games, Iowa State University, Department of Economics Working Paper No 17922

Tisdell, C. and S. Svizzero, 2015, Rent Extraction, Population Growth and Economic Development: Development despite Malthus' theory and precursors to the Industrial Revolution, The University of Queensland, Economic Theory, Applications and Issues Working Paper No 73

Turner, P., 2011, Is the long-term interest rate a policy victim, a policy variable or a policy lodestar? BIS Working Paper No. 367

Tymoigne, E., 2008, Minsky and Economic Policy: "Keynesianism" All Over Again? Levy Economics Institute of Bard College Working Paper No 47

Ugolini, S., 2011, What do we really know about the long-term evolution of central banking? Evidence from the past, insights for the present, Norges Bank Working Paper 2011/15

Vozna, L., 2016, How Economists can use the Laws of Physics: On the example of the Notion of Entropy in its Application to the Some Economic Conceptions, STOREPapers, Italian Association for the History of Political Economy Working Paper 1-2016

Vredin, A., 2015, Inflation targeting and financial stability: providing policy makers with relevant information, BIS Working Paper No 503

Wallis, P., J. Colson and D. Chilosi, 2016, Puncturing the Malthusian delusion: Structural change in the British economy before the industrial revolution, 1500-1800, The London School of Economics and Political Science, Economic History Working Paper No 240/2016

Weber, W. E., 2015, Government and Private e Money-Like Systems: Federal Reserve Notes and National Bank Notes, Bank of Canada Working Paper 2015-18

White, W.R., 2013, Is Monetary Policy Still a Science? Federal Reserve Bank of Dallas, Globalization and Monetary Policy Institute Working Paper No 155

Williamson, S.D., 2015, Current Federal Reserve Policy Under the Lens of Economic History, Federal Reserve Bank of St Luis Research Division Working Paper 2015—15A

Wray, L. R., 2011, Is There Room for Bulls, Bears, and States in the Circuit? Levy Economics Institute of Bard College Working Paper No 700

__________, 2012, A Meme for Money, Levy Economics Institute of Bard College Working Paper No 736

__________, 2015, Chapter 7: Minsky's approach to prudent banking and the evolution of the financial system, Reforming the Fed's Policy Response in the Era of Shadow Banking, Ford Foundation, Levy Economics Institute of Bard College

Wray, L.R., and X. Liu., 2014, Options for China in a Dollar Standard: A Sovereign Currency, Jerome Levy Economics Institute of Bard College Working Paper No 783

Index

S

T

W

www.ingramcontent.com/pod-product-compliance
Lightning Source LLC
LaVergne TN
LVHW010721210926
848485LV00007B/1401/J
* 9 7 8 1 6 2 2 7 3 1 8 1 7 *